ART BY CARL LAVOIE

Vastarien

A Literary Journal

Volume Seven, Issue Zero

Jon Padgett, Editor-in-Chief

Paula D. Ashe, Associate Editor

Daniel Braum, Associate Editor

Alex Jennings, Associate Editor

New Orleans, Louisiana

© 2024 Grimscribe Press

Cover design by Anna Trueman

Unless noted, all internal art by Dave Felton

All rights reserved. No part of this publication may be reproduced, distributed, or transmitted in any form or by any means, including photocopying, recording, or other electronic or mechanical methods, without the prior written permission of the publisher, except in the case of brief quotations embodied in critical reviews and certain other noncommercial uses permitted by copyright law.

Published by
Grimscribe Press
New Orleans, LA
USA

grimscribepress.com

Acknowledgments	i
Vastarien Column: Tenebrous Ramblings *Romana Lockwood*	1
Molly on the Stairhead *Richard Gavin*	5
Ekphrasis *M.E. Bronstein*	19
Five Poems *Marisca Pichette*	35
Winter Blues *Laura Cranehill*	41
The Dance of Life (After Edvard Munch) *Adam Lawrence*	55
An Angel of God *Emma E. Murray*	57
Tonight, the Moon is not Quite Complete *SJ Townend*	67

Extinction *Alyza Taguilaso*	83
Auntie Shanta and the Slaughtering Process *Chris Kuriata*	85
The Dark Wood Teaman *Rebecca J. Allred*	95
Labyrinthine *Michael Bailey*	111
Everything Wrong with Me *Carson Winter*	123
The Great Everything of Dust *César Dávila Andrade* *(translated by Jonathan Simkins)*	135
Acts of Desperation *César Dávila Andrade* *(translated by Jonathan Simkins)*	137
The People Upstairs *Ben Larned*	139
The City Archives *Paul L. Bates*	151
These Graceless, Grasping Hands *Dyani Sabin*	163

The Flytrap Garden *Perry Ruhland*	165
The Place, The People, The Predators: The Ligottian World of Vancouver's Downtown Eastside *Shawn Phelps*	173
A Wild Green Tide is Soon Coming — Notes on a Planned Story *Jonathan Louis Duckworth*	183
Learning Process *Andrew Wilbur*	193
Contributors	201

ACKNOWLEDGMENTS

Thanks to all our benefactors, particularly James Michael Baker, Samuel Cottrill, Matthew Henshaw, and Tyson Sereda.

ART BY ISOTTA SANTINELLI

Tenebrous Ramblings

by Romana Lockwood

I am writing this column from roughly five feet under the earth, four yards from the bulkhead of my house.

I am draped in darkness and melancholy. And disappointment. I should have seen this coming. When I was younger, I would have.

Of course, I'm not writing this column in any real sense. I'm sending it psychically to Dr. Scan, my psychic-iatrist, if you will. My hope is that he will receive it, commit it to paper, contact suitable friends and entities, and thereby set into motion a rescue.

It is not assured he will receive it. I've always sent my messages to his mind from above ground.

We are on—under—untested ground.

As you recall from my last column, I had hired Myrna George, a retired schoolteacher, to be my live-in carer. I met her son, who clothed himself like a Halloween store cowboy, and despite my concerns (shallowly based upon his appearance), he was reserved, quiet, and sweetly protective of his mother. He had insisted on meeting me in order to see whether he thought it was a good fit. I played the role of the slightly dotty, fading (who am I kidding, *faded)* ingenue. Maybe if I hadn't been concentrating upon my performance, I would have seen the signs.

The meeting went well.

Of course it did.

The son and a gang of taciturn, tattooed men delivered and unloaded some of her furniture and effects. They hauled them with some effort and a lot of cursing to the upstairs set of rooms I'd prepared for her. These were the sort of humorless, hard men whose cursing seems a precursor to violence. I was on edge during the hour and a half they were in my house. I feared I'd made a mistake.

Taking on a carer involves a good deal of orientation. They must learn to know your preferences, your ways, that which you prefer, that which you can bear if you must, and that which you will not tolerate under any circumstances. You must show them where everything is and expect them to commit much of it to memory and learn the rest quickly. You have to tell them the specific brands you wish them to purchase at the supermarket, and the quantity of each. This was a learning experience for me as well; I knew what I wanted and somehow at first I just assumed Ms. George would know that as well.

Trial and error.

The first sign of trouble came on a very windy evening when Ms. George prepared my bath and helped me into the tub. She left the room on some pretense the nature of which I don't recall. I quickly discovered that my soap bar was as thin as a wafer. I couldn't reach a new bar. I called out to her. I heard rummaging coming from below—not furtive, but as though performed with frustration and anger. Had she gone into the basement? I hadn't specifically forbade it, but it was locked—from below. I called out again, louder. I heard footsteps ascending the basement steps.

Ms. George appeared in the doorway. Her typical kindly expression was gone, replaced with sheer blind blankness. Her face and head were festooned with dust and hair. A low growl came from her, not from her mouth, but from her chest, or belly. "Ms. George," I said, moderating my tone, for I was in an extraordinarily vulnerable state, "I must insist that you please refrain from entering the basement or the attic, unless I specifically request something from..." and as I spoke, I felt my tone getting harsher, increasingly loud and shrill.

The water in which I reclined suddenly grew very cold—cold and rapidly getting colder until it stung like frostbite. To my terror, the water began to *invade my body*. "Well, that's fine, of course," I said quickly, babbling a little, "no harm done. I'm so... I'm so very glad you're here."

She flinched as though a small firecracker had popped just at her ear. She nodded her head abruptly and the kindly expression returned to her face—it was like a welder's mask dropping into place. The water bubbled from my body (such incredible relief) and the tub grew warmer. For a moment I feared it would keep warming until I boiled to death in my own home.

"Certainly, ma'am," came her reply, cold as the water had been, despite the warmth of her expression.

She did not get me a fresh bar of soap. She backed out of the bathroom slowly and jerkily, gazing warmly upon me as she did. I washed as best as I could and called for her to assist getting me out of the tub and dried off, which she did silently, but gently and efficiently. She had removed the dust from her head, I noticed. Later, me in my robe, her in her sweats, we sat for television—Ms. George seemed interested in the British police drama I was watching and asked questions about the characters and their histories. She asked if I should like some tea. And so, we sipped our tea and sat in such a way that a disinterested observer might reasonably think was companionable.

I was shaking inside. I was considering stealing away to contact one of my cohorts. Would that I had done so. I waited for her to fall asleep. She didn't. Somewhere into the third episode I started and woke in my bed. I felt very sleepy. Perhaps unnaturally so. I tried to push myself up but was weak. I tried to call to her, to have her take my temperature, but my voice wouldn't rise above a whisper. Finally, I fell back on my pillows. I fancied that the door was open just a crack—a half-rectangle of dark, dark blue against the blackness—and that Ms. George was watching me.

Taking my measure.

Planning.

Molly on the Stairhead

Richard Gavin

Y OU'VE PROBABLY NEVER played Molly on the Stairhead. Few people have, though everyone knows some variation of it; Bloody Mary being the most obvious example, but really any of the folk games involving mirrors and the incanting of bloodstained ghosts would qualify. These slumber party rituals designed to conjure spectral terrors in a mirror have fascinated me since I was a teenager. I've studied them for years, but the explanations offered by psychologists and anthropologists always feel superficial, reductionist. Even the theories that I like, such as that these activities are forms of female adolescent initiation for a secularized world, where we girls can draw upon fear and gory apparitions so we can begin to accept our menstrual cycle, still only circumambulate the truth. With all respect to Dr. Freud, even these taboo notions barely scratch the looking-glass surface of the issue.

I believe that these activities do initiate young people into truths about life, but the truths conveyed through Molly on the Stairhead cannot be accepted, not fully, not if the recipient wants to hang onto even the thinnest threads of their sanity. This game is rooted in reality, and reality is not sane. I know whereof I speak because I knew Molly. What's more, I was there the night she first encountered the terror that lurks at the top of the stairs.

Molly and I had been friends since kindergarten. Our bond endured grade school, though it was apparent even back then that Molly had willingly or unwillingly been fated to an unhealthily permanent childhood. During our freshman year of high school, I was nowhere near as worldly or rebellious as I wanted to believe, but Molly was embarrassingly stunted in every way; intellectually, physically, and emotionally. It was almost as if she had seen womanhood and all that it entails waiting for her around the bend and opted instead to try and swim backwards against the current, to insinuate herself back onto that island of childhood from which she (and all of us) had been jettisoned. Where I forced myself into feigning lust for boys and a thirst for liquor and a hankering for cigarettes, Molly seemed bent on endlessly haunting the wild spaces where she and I had spent lazy, dull summer afternoons as children, those imaginary queendoms that we'd once sworn to protect with secret handshakes and whispered passwords.

Her favorite locale (mine too, if I'm honest) was the Greens: a mid-size patch of woodlands that some giant development company bought long ago and fenced-in but never did anything with. As you might imagine, just as the Greens was an ideal place for afternoon games, it was equally utilized nocturnally by teenagers looking to throw themselves into high-risk situations. This was especially true for girls.

One random Thursday in the early fall, a group of my newer acquaintances conspired to sneak out of our homes for illicit festivities in the Greens. Molly's invitation had been extended at my insistence. Throughout that first semester I had seen her brutally punished and ostracized by our peers because of her bratty antics, her defiant, obnoxious childishness. My new closest friend Nan was there that night. Three boys came with us too, but they don't matter, neither then nor now. At that time, Nan and I had convinced ourselves that two of them had the makings of acceptable boyfriends. We'd presumed the third could be paired off with Molly if the spirit moved them.

Our rendezvous point was the not-so-clandestine tear in the chain-link fence that framed the Greens. This opening was known to everyone in town, and was landmarked by a lonely, grime-encrusted payphone bolted to a wooden post.

Molly was late, of course, and her appearance was met with a chorus of hyena laughter from everyone but me. She had come attired in a formal party dress: pink satin made bulbous with white crinoline that pulsed like sea amoebas beneath her skirt every time she moved. It was the sort of thing a little girl might wear to match her favorite doll.

She came traipsing across the dewy, knee-high grass, the white lace trim iridescent in the darkness. She was smiling broadly, and I wondered if she mistook the group's mockery for glee over her presence. Red lipstick (borrowed from her mother's purse, no doubt) stained her teeth. Her saddle shoes, into which her broad feet had been painfully stuffed, were caked with mud. The moon reflected off her glasses.

Somebody peeled back the severed fence, and we stole into the Greens. One of the boys didn't bother to hold the fence for Molly, and she yelped when some of the severed fence wires bit into her calf. I helped her up, now feeling heartsick for my friend, seeing just how out of her element she was.

"I'm being punished," she whispered to me as she fingered the bloody puncture marks in her white knee-high socks.

Nan passed around a flask of peppermint schnapps, and someone else lit up some cannabis. I was unhealthily proud when I saw Molly accept the joint, but instead of inhaling its smoke she daydreamed over the burning tip for a few seconds, as though it was a firefly she'd caught between her fingers. When she passed the joint onto me, there were bloodstains on the rolling paper.

We wandered deeper into the trees. Nan and I both seemed to be enjoying the feeling of being wanted by the boys we were with. Molly hobbled along at the end of our party, not saying a word.

Exactly who heard the staircase moving towards us I cannot recall, but whoever it was quickly alerted the others, and soon our entourage instinctively formed a crescent pattern at the edge of a clearing. We stared awe-struck at the impossibility before us.

It emerged slowly from the trees on the far edge of the clearing, moving silently, like a carved glacier slicing through green waters. It was a grand marble staircase: alabaster veined with thin swirls of pale grey, like wisps of smoke. Fat balusters that resembled Grecian vases lined each step. The bannisters were broad and shined as if newly polished. The bottommost step was bearded with ryegrass and dappled with sparkling beads of dew. The stairhead was level with the treetops.

It was the kind of fixture you'd imagine inside a castle or an old-world opera house. Queens or princes would come down those steps, surrounded by loyal subjects. At first, I thought it might have been part of a ruin, a relic of a mansion that had been on the Greens before the land was bought, but there was no foundation, no nothing. Just the staircase, moving to greet us for some unfathomable reason.

For a long time, we simply stared at it, none of us truly seeing it. How could we? To see is to recognize, and we could only recognize pieces (billowing evergreens, harvest moon, grand staircase) but not the whole scene, because the whole scene simply could not be. We were frightened, and being young, we dealt with our fear by denying it. The jokes began, as did threats of defacing or destroying the staircase, all in the voice of fragile male egos. Molly never uttered a sound.

I was the first one to suggest that someone climb it, as ashamed as I am to admit that now. Naturally, *I* had no intention of doing the deed. Secretly, I wanted Molly to go, wanted her to feel impelled, by peer pressure or something supernatural it did not matter.

"She goes first," one of the boys commanded above the din, pointing a dirty finger at Molly. I'd gotten my wish, and Molly complied without protest.

She looked so tiny scaling those polished steps in her party dress, surrounded by woods, crowned with a lustrous moon. The scene was a collision of two worlds, the opulent and the savage, like something out of a dream or a visionary painting.

When she reached the stairhead, Molly turned to face us. She said something, but none of us heard what it was. She removed her hand from the banister, took a regressive step, and to our collective horror, fell backward from the top of the stairs.

One of the boys bellowed "No!" while another cursed. Nan and I screamed Molly's name in unison. All of us heard her land. Her body hit the ground with a sickening thump, along with the awful, unmistakable burst of glass being shattered.

I was the first one to rush to the staircase, terrified of what I would find there. I kept my hands balled up at my stomach to avoid accidentally touching the tomb-like marble. I was shaking so badly I could hardly walk, and when I called Molly's name my voice was the peep of a frightened mouse. When my call went unanswered, I forced myself to peek behind the staircase.

A fractured mirror was the only thing lying in the mud. Like the staircase, the mirror was large and opulent, with a great carved frame adorned with goldleaf. Its full-length looking glass was nested in an arabesque frame. The glass had shattered into a perfect cobweb pattern whose white veins were flecked with fresh blood. It was weirdly pretty. Several silver shards had also been flung over the ground from the impact. They too bore a stippling of young blood.

Molly was nowhere to be seen. She was simply gone. Like the staircase suddenly appearing, Molly had suddenly disappeared. Our party, sobered by panic, scoured the Greens from one end to the other. We called for Molly until our throats were shredded. Our search eventually led us back to the staircase, which loomed as if it was daring another of us to scale it.

By then the air had grown frigid and damp. The grasses were heavy with dew. We began to argue over whether to go to the police or to spin an elaborate alibi that would remove us from the tangles of Molly's disappearance. Naturally, we took the cowardly route, each of us swearing to absolute secrecy. We crept back to the aperture by the payphone and went our separate ways.

I carried myself home on weak legs, and when I finally crept back into my waiting bed, I cried until the sun rose. That morning felt like the beginning of the end of everything, but of course it wasn't. Oh, there were panic and tears as news of Molly's disappearance spread like wildfire through the town. But the longer the investigation went on, the more obvious it became that her vanishing would remain unsolved, and that neither myself nor any of my peers who'd been there that night would ever be suspected.

The narrative was that Molly had been abducted from her bed, where she'd been sleeping the sleep of the just. Her bedroom window had been found slightly ajar, and because Molly was such a naïve and well-behaved girl, the notion that she'd snuck out of her own accord was quickly dismissed by her parents and eventually by the police.

I was questioned, but so was the entire student body. I confirmed that yes, I'd known Molly for most of my life, and no, I couldn't think of anyone who might have wanted to hurt her. Daily search parties crisscrossed the town, but their beating of the bushes yielded nothing. Nan and I were part of the first group to move through the Greens, and when our party reached that fateful clearing, there was no trace of the marble stairs or the broken mirror.

What happened next? Life went on. As it does. As it must. One by one the tv station vans departed and Molly's supposed abduction went from being front-page news to the occasional column tucked between human-interest stories and grocery ads. A memorial shrine was erected around the oak tree on Molly's front lawn, all sorts of flowers swathed in vibrant cellophane, children's drawings that became illegible after a few rainfalls, statuary, little placards that assured passersby of a life eternal. I was always amazed by those kinds of convictions; people who barely understood what made themselves tick seemed to be the first ones to offer guarantees about the unseen.

I distracted myself with my studies, and through the winter I avoided socializing with my peers by taking babysitting jobs for my parents' friends. My grades were not great, but they were decent, and I felt a certain warmth in my chest over making good life choices. Molly would have been proud of me.

The Addison twins were my most frequent charges. They lived in a large colonial house just a few blocks away. Their mother worked in the same engineering firm as my father. The pittance I earned minding the twins was hard-earned. They were not badly behaved, but they were peculiar, so much so that being around them for too long gave me generalized anxiety. The boys were constantly whispering amongst themselves, tittering at private jokes, or challenging me with senseless riddles of their own invention.

None of the neighborhood children bothered with the Addison boys, and I suppose that made me pity them and want to be especially kind to them. In many ways they reminded me of Molly.

On the night of the company Christmas party, I thought the twins might enjoy a change of scenery, so I bundled them up and trundled them over to my empty house. The glee they burst with when they saw the Christmas tree in my living room was contagious, and I basically gave them free reign. They explored my house as if it were some fabulous vault of treasures. After bouncing on my bed for awhile, they asked if they could play in our basement.

"Won't you be scared down there?" I asked them, "I sure would be."

The brothers shook their heads emphatically. I told them that if they pinky-swore not to touch anything down there, they could play for twenty minutes, then it was time for pajamas and whatever animated Christmas special happened to be airing that night.

My spirits stayed high as I listened to the boys giggling and jabbering to each other through the furnace vents in the kitchen floor. I heated a tinfoil pan of popcorn, and when this noisy chore was done, I suddenly appreciated how quiet the house had become. The basement door, which I'd propped open while the boys played, was now closed. The lights had been switched off.

"Boys?" I called in a voice as shaky as my hands. "Boys!" I leaned my ear to the basement door. The familiar Addison twins whisper was faintly audible through the flimsy wood. The relief I felt from this shattered once I was able to discern the words being rasped:

"Molly's on the stairhead,
Molly's in the trees,
Molly's in the mirror,
Molly's after me!"

The boys repeated the phrase over and over, like a chant. Their two-person chorus grew louder and more frenzied with each repetition. The sound of Molly's name froze me in-place for what felt like hours. Finally, I mustered the courage to fling open the basement door, which caused the boys to scream blue murder from the bottom of the stairs where they were huddled.

When I saw the dark figure standing before them, I also screamed. On instinct, my hand slapped the light switch. The light allowed me to see that the figure I'd screamed at was my own reflection. The boys, despite their pinky-swear, had unearthed an old medicine chest with a mirror door, which my parents must have stashed down there when they'd renovated the main bathroom years earlier. I slumped down on the landing and broke down in tears. The Addison boys were even more hysterical. I ushered them into the cozier surroundings of the living room. When their hysteria finally abated, I asked them what it was they thought they were doing down there.

"Playing Molly on the Stairhead," one mumbled. The other nodded to validate his brother's claim.

It was on the tip of my tongue to ask how they knew about Molly, but fortunately my rational mind reined me in. Her name and her face had been ubiquitous around town just a few months ago, so it's entirely plausible that the boys could have absorbed a few details about her, even subconsciously. And who was to say it was even the same Molly?

I asked them to tell me where they'd learned that game.

"We just knew how," mumbled one brother, "it was easy."

At my insistence, they explained the rules.

"You get a mirror," the other twin began, pronouncing the last word as 'me-war,' "and then you make everything all dark and then you sit at the end of some stairs and then you tell the mirror to bring you Molly and then Molly comes."

"And what does Molly do?" I rasped, not truly wanting the answer.

Both boys instantly regressed before my eyes, each inserting their thumb into their mouth, and curling up on either end of the sofa like toddlers. I told them that I wasn't buying their playing possum, but I was unnerved to find that they truly had fallen asleep just like that. Dread must have short-circuited their young brains, and they simply shut down from the world. Once they were asleep, I slipped into the basement to retrieve the old medicine chest, which I tossed into the trash can behind our garage. I never babysat for the Addisons again.

The following day I began to lose things. At first the missing objects were so insignificant I scarcely noticed their absence: a bus ticket, the cover for my favorite mixed tape, a few random socks. The first incident to cause me any real distress was when my housekeys vanished from my purse. I turned my entire house upside down hunting for them. They never did turn up, but even this loss was remedied by the spare set that my parents kept hanging in our front hall.

I began to question why it is that people accept vanishment so easily. Trivial losses are of course seen as simply a part of life, as if the banishment of objects into a void are sane occurrences. Oh, we indulge in a bit of mania as we ransack of our own homes, but just when we are beginning to sense how egregious this kind of violation of natural law truly is, some default in our biology is always there to talk us down off the proverbial ledge. Then, like all good victims of systemic gaslighting and abuse, we blame ourselves for being absentminded and wait for the scales of cosmic order to tilt back into balance, and by doing so we rob ourselves of the dreadful awareness of cosmic wrongness that is our birthright.

My experience in the Greens severed the cord that kept me tethered to surety, but Christmas Day that year was when I realized just how far I had drifted. My parents and I were huddled around the tree that the Addison twins had so admired. We were exchanging presents and doing our utmost to milk the holiday for any joy it could offer after an autumn of pain and confusion. Our efforts seemed to be working, but my enjoyment ended when my mother pulled a strange bundle out from under the tree and showed that my name was written in perfect calligraphy on the tag.

"Mel, is that from you?" mumbled my mother to my father. He shook his head and shrugged his shoulders.

I accepted the parcel, which wasn't giftwrapped but loosely covered in a sack of yellow satin. The fabric was musty and bore several ugly brown stains. I disliked the gritty coating that the knotted cord left on my fingers as I contended with it, and when I finally unveiled my mysterious present, I became catatonic for a few seconds until some primordial survival instinct forced me to smile and be delighted with the antique mirror whose restored glass reflected my shock-paled face back at me.

"Who on Earth gave you that?" asked my mother.

"Nan," was my instant lie, "we saw it in an antique store during a field trip. She must have gone back into the city to buy it for me. I'll have to call later and say thank you."

The true answer to my mother's question was that no one *on Earth* had given me the mirror. I hadn't spoken to Nan in months, but I wasn't lying when I'd said I would be calling the sender of my gift.

In the wee hours I took the opulent mirror with me to the basement. I positioned it so that the entire staircase was reflected, then I switched off the light.

My eyes took a long time to adjust, but gradually I was able to divine my own silhouette perched on the bottommost step, along with the merest hint of the stairhead above me. I suppose I was waiting for some kind of sign to tell me it was time to begin, but none seemed forthcoming, and my anxiety was starting to overwhelm me, so I quietly incanted:

"Molly's on the stairhead,
Molly's in the trees…"

My whisper seemed thunderous against the absolute stillness of my house, and a chill quivered down my back. I wasn't sure if I had nerve enough to continue.

*"Molly's in the mirror,
Molly's after me..."*

One of the steps behind me creaked. A pale wisp skittered across the surface of the mirror. My heartbeat grew so frantic I feared I might be having a stroke. I only noticed I was crying after I felt the warm splash of my tears on my hands, which were gripping my bent knees, trying to keep them stable.

I repeated the menacing rhyme, still whispered, but this time with more ferocity. The words gushed out in a sibilant hiss, more akin to a curse than a calling. Immediately after the second round, the temperature in the basement plummeted. There were four creaks on the stairs this time, and the looking glass shone brightly for a few seconds, as though it was casting the reflection of a waxing moon.

After the fifth cycle of the chant, Molly appeared on the stairhead. Her time in the afterlife had altered her. She was still attired in the same birthday-cake-like party dress, but her body was horribly elongated, and her head was grossly enlarged. Her reflection petrified me, almost literally. I now know whereof the ancient Greek myths spoke when they warned of a person being turned to stone by the merest glimpse of the Gorgon. Molly was ably filling the role of my personal Medusa.

I could see her jaundiced eyes reflected in the looking-glass, bulging from their sockets like boils on the verge of bursting. The stairway felt positively airless, as if the atmosphere of the basement was holding its breath in stunned awe over Molly on the Stairhead. My head began to swim. My peripheral vision became filled with pale ripples that were almost luminous in contrast to the darkness that enveloped me. These white ribbons affected me queerly. I began to feel giddy.

Molly must have been sharing in my deranged glee, for I saw her great face mangle to form a grin. This movement conjured a rattling noise, a jangling caused by the shards of mirror that had replaced her teeth. The insertion of the looking-glass pieces must have been excruciating, but the torture did not diminish Molly's childish mirth. Her lanky, looming shape began to shake with silent laughter. The silvery fangs glittered and clacked, and the pale ropy things in my periphery seemed to draw nearer.

It wasn't until they lunged forward and gripped my head that I realized those whitish shapes were not hallucinations. They had heft and a humbling might. They were Molly's fingers clinging to me like creeping vines. I tried to scream, and Molly took advantage of my gaping mouth. She slid her fingers deep into my throat and stole my voice. Her nimble fingers snapped back up the steps, my voice pinched between them. I watched Molly fall backwards, just as she had done on that grand staircase in the Greens, and just like that night, she disappeared.

My parents discovered me the next morning, huddled at the base of the stairs, my body haloed by pieces of a broken mirror. Their initial fears that I had fallen down the steps were assuaged after I was admitted to the hospital. I was physically intact and psychologically lucid, but nevertheless, I was altered. According to the psychiatrists who examined me, I was still perfectly capable of speaking, but I had, for some mysterious reason, drifted into selective mutism.

"Once we pinpoint the trauma at the root of this condition," one of the psychiatrists assured my distraught parents, "we can begin to treat it, and then the odds are very promising that your daughter will be her old self again."

That carrot of encouragement had been dangled before my parents nearly forty years ago. Now they and the doctor who spoke those words are long dead, and in all that time I haven't been able to reclaim my voice. I'm grateful for journaling, since it has allowed me to communicate, if only to myself. Having the illusion of an orderly, plot-like life is a pleasant thing.

Every now and again, Molly allows me to find my voice, but always perversely, always in the form of some twisted game. She'll stash my voice where she knows I'm sure to come across it, like a mother hiding Easter eggs for their child in plain sight to keep them engaged in the hunt, but the places she chooses are always scary and strange.

Molly on the Stairhead

One night on one of my frequent pilgrimages to the Greens (the staircase never did reappear), I heard the decrepit payphone ringing incessantly. Reluctantly, I moved to it and pulled the filthy receiver from its mount. I stood listening to my own voice maundering frantically. I was so desperate to reclaim my voice that I tried to inhale it as though it was smoke. It eluded me of course, and then it began the chant of Molly on the Stairhead.

Molly appeared. She always does. She's come to play with me so often over the years that her appearance is almost mundane. Almost.

What keeps my frequent encounters with her fresh and startling are the aberrations she reveals to me. If Molly has taught me one thing (and I like to think she's taught me much), it is that Death's house has many mansions. Prior to this ordeal, which I fell into as surely as Molly did, I suppose my view of Death was that it was either an endless nothingness or a place where I'd be reacquainted with the ghosts of people that I'd lost. It never really occurred to me that the land of the Dead could be just as bad, if not worse, than earthly existence. A believer would be tempted to pounce on this theory and say that what I'm describing here is Hell. It isn't. Hell has a purpose. I don't think many theologians would accept that not all our dear departed attain a state of grace once they pass through from being into non-being, nor do they receive their rightful punishment. Instead, some play with a puckish zeal for misrule.

It is eternity as a temper tantrum, the afterlife as a cheap spook-house on a derelict midway. Life circles back in on itself. Maybe Death brings out the brat in everyone, and that's why Molly excels there, living her best afterlife in the chaos of phantoms and endless distortion.

Geriatrics are often praised for their child-like innocence, and maybe this is how we know our time has come; we forget how to be adults and begin a slippery, inexorable slide down the bannisters of some phantom staircase. I once read that the bodies of coma patients will instinctively begin to curl up into a fetal position; the nearly dead preparing themselves as newborns shifting into a lunatic nursery.

How could it be any way other than this? After all, we start playing the game not long after we are born; the first paradox that is thrust upon us, the first painful loss that we are told by our elders is something we simply must accept. Some things are hidden and never found, other things that should not be manifest spontaneously; a spectral staircase floats in and a young girl falls into a crack between worlds. It all feels wrong, like a great machine that's not been properly assembled; it functions, but noisily and with frequent kinks and system failures.

I will not poison your mind with some of the aberrations that Molly has ferried into my world from hers. I don't know how many more of her miracles I can bear. The game has exhausted me. It's as if I'm still that frightened young babysitter watching the Addison twins tug at the fraying Veil.

For years I've silently pleaded with Molly to take my eyes. I no longer want to see. But I know she'd just lodge them in the face of some monstrosity and then tear away my eyelids, forcing me to see what it is not meant to be seen, forever and ever. So, I go on, passing each day like it's a step on an unseen staircase. I hope I find the stairhead. I'm waiting for the fall. Perhaps on the other side of the mirror I will find my voice at last. But I'm terribly afraid of what I'll have to say.

Ekphrasis

M.E. Bronstein

Ana Sarkis
American, 1987-2015
Echoes of Sea Sounds, 2015
Graphite and ink on paper

In this homage to Romantic landscape painting, a solitary young woman (perhaps a stand-in for the artist herself) stares out at a turbulent sea as a storm gathers in the distance. Sarkis's oeuvre is full of contemplative figures transfixed by bodies of water—a motif which certain (perhaps over-zealous) critics have read in connection with the artist's unfortunate death by drowning. The composition distinctly echoes Caspar David Friedrich's Monk by the Sea.

George and Ana met while he was working on his article for *Skiagraphia*. Specks of stray ink freckled her studio's pale floorboards. She had lots of bowls and fountains and birdbaths and fans propped up on stools to make the water ripple (reference material, Ana said). She opened up portfolios and spread drawings and paintings across a table for him.

Her chaotic linework became more elegant, though no more intelligible, the closer he looked. George scribbled a thing down about how it "bordered on textuality." A tangle of branches looked like an ampersand, messy pseudo-script marked an open book, a parenthetical sliver of moon framed alphabetic constellations. Almost but never quite readable.

Ana showed him works in progress: faded grays and bursts of gold. She'd start with dense graphite, then erase and riddle her leftover shadows with bright inks. She said, "It's like memory." Returning to the past brings out some details while others blur, and so on.

Ana had a strange glass pen—it looked like the kind of thing a fancy stationery store would put in the window but nobody would really use.

Ana used it. She dipped it in a jar of gold ink, and then new highlights rippled across a sketch of a birdbath. Her hand darted back and forth, almost shaped real letters, then didn't. George tracked her progress hungrily, until he noticed something—like fireflies, sparklers—winking through the dim in the corner of his eye. An echo in the studio's air of Ana's linework? But the glitter vanished whenever he tried to find it. "Ana...?" he said, then trailed off, mesmerized all over again by her pen's dance.

Ana stopped working and made for a window. She hauled up the sash, fished a cigarette out of her pocket, and gestured for George to come join her.

"Well? What do you think?" she said. "Enough fodder for that article of yours?"

He inched closer, admired the stripe of dull gold that fell across the curve of her cheek—a reflection of the streetlamps as they stained the air outside with grimy light.

"Yep," he said, and something in his voice got a smile out of her, and a dimple wrinkled the light on her skin.

Ana spent the next few evenings cross-legged on George's floor; she'd study the ice in her glass of bourbon while he sorted through sketches spread across his coffee table.

"You're not messing with me?" she asked him, again and again. "You're into it? Sometimes I don't think this stuff should make sense to anyone who's not me."

He reassured her. It wasn't that her work "made sense" to him, but it "spoke" to him—whatever that meant. Not that he'd object if she ever wanted to share more of her process, the logic of it. Now to ask about her inspiration without sounding like a dope. He settled on: "You have any reference material I could see?"

Ana said, "Kind of."

The next time he visited her studio, she showed him old albums, tugged a Polaroid out of its sleeve. A photo of the East River. A younger Ana perched at the edge of a pier and stared at nothing. Black water and a shadow of the Brooklyn Bridge swallowed up most of the picture plane. George mistook the flecks of pale gold light scattered across the photo for dust at first; he tried and failed to wipe it clean. Ana had scrawled a date in the corner: August 14th, 2003.

"The blackout?" said George.

"You remember?"

"Well—the chaos of it, yes. Too soon after 9/11."

"Never thought of it that way," said Ana, frowning.

She and her friends wound up in Dumbo by the water, listened to the East River rush and mutter against the ferry landing. It was the only time Ana ever saw stars in the city—stars in the sky and stars in the water. She could hear people freaking out through the night. All that loud loneliness felt very alien just then. Another lifetime. Ana thought about jumping into the water but didn't.

George almost laughed; he could see her wanting to become part of the scene—to swim among reflected stars.

"I wish I could still be there," she said. "I wish that memory hadn't ended."

"Then it wouldn't be a memory," said George. "That's what makes it beautiful, right?"

Ana said, "I don't know." She slipped her headphones back on and returned to her work.

Her barriers were already beginning to irk him. Later, after they had spent maybe an hour in each other's company without exchanging a word, he knelt and pressed his ear to hers, tried to listen. She laughed and shoved him away.

And he struggled to figure out what he'd heard: not music at all, but a faint hiss and murmur, like waves ebbing and crashing.

A review of a poorly-attended show called Ana's drawings "layered but messy"—"Sarkis's visual allusions to familiar myths are far more compelling than her oftentimes abstruse efforts to mythologize her own history…"

George promised he would write something better, something that would "do her justice."

He wrote about how she embodied an ekphrastic playfulness: "Ekphrasis—an elaborate, visually charged piece of description, often of an invented art object—reflects a text's effort to wield control over an image, describing it so vividly that it seems to move, to speak, and articulate itself. Sarkis operates the other way around. The strange almost-textuality of her work grants her subjects their own eerie vivacity…" He had the glass pen in mind but didn't write about it. Pygmalion's ekphrastic chisel, that could write inert art to life.

Unless he had dreamed that into it. He wondered sometimes.

Ana frowned at the article, kept fiddling with greasy strands of hair that had strayed from her bun. She slouched over her kitchen table, ripples shifting across her ivory nightshirt (stained a little around the pits). The last few times he had come to see her, she hadn't bothered getting dressed.

As she let the last page fall to the table, Ana studied George in silence, and then a short laugh boiled out of her.

"What?" George asked.

"I'm glad you're writing about me," she admitted.

Or, no—didn't she say something different, a little more stinging? More like: "Now I see why you're so eager to write about me."

In one of her darkest moods, Ana tore several pages out of her sketchbook and glutted his garbage disposal. She kept daring George to convince her that her abilities weren't just in her head (or in both of their heads). And so George introduced Ana to colleagues, to critics and curators, did his best to plant her name in their heads too. It seldom took.

Ana's more difficult tics surfaced whenever George asked her to describe her work. A lot of hedging, "sort of" this and "kind of" that. When people asked her questions, she'd often answer with a shrug or an "I don't know," freeze like she sensed a trick question at an oral exam.

George liked to think of his job as humbling. He had heard translators describe their process that way—and wasn't art criticism a kind of translation, just between media rather than languages? In either case, the idea was to bury your own ego, to uplift another creator's work.

But whenever George stepped in and explained on Ana's behalf, she would stiffen, figure out an excuse to pull them both away. Later, she would say, "George. These people don't get it—don't *want* to get it. This isn't helping."

But he had to help. He needed to show her just how much he could help.

He decided to surprise Ana with the kind of show she deserved. He wrote out the gallery labels himself, using Ana's own pen and golden ink.

Had it been intentional, on some level? Or just thoughtless?

All George ever wanted was to uplift Ana. He never imagined that the pen would obey him, too. (Again, the needling question about her talent and wherever it was really located—had she just tapped into something by accident, that she didn't understand any better than he did?)

George arranged her favorite pieces throughout his apartment. Some of the labels were serious, others silly, stuffed with invented details about an illustrious career that Ana had yet to lead. He even wrote a playful allusion to a tragic, youthful death that would earn her everlasting fame. That kind of macabre drama usually got a laugh out of her.

Their friends arrived. George poured prosecco and played the tour guide.

And then Ana herself appeared. She stood in the doorway and the crowd drunkenly applauded her. George took her limp hand, steered her through the apartment and showed her his handiwork.

But it was like Ana—liquid, elusive Ana—had turned to stone. He had never seen that look on her face before. Petrification. Mortification? One of those.

"Well," said George, "what do you think?"

She didn't answer. He was about to repeat himself when she stumbled and leaned against the nearest wall, her body stuttering. It took a moment to grasp that she was laughing—quietly, yet harder than George had ever seen her laugh. At first she couldn't talk around her mirth. But then, somehow, she managed. She said, "George, you doofus."

"Excuse me?" After all he had done for her.

"How am I going to fix this?" she said.

"Fix what?"

A couple of George's older colleagues gathered to say nice things about Ana's progress. Ana answered in monosyllables, then muttered that she needed a smoke and wormed away.

George's protests died half-uttered. He felt wounded, though unsurprised, when she didn't return to the party, which she had probably misconstrued as some kind of mockery of her aspirations rather than the playful prophecy he had intended.

He found his room—where he had let guests fling their coats and bags—upturned, his desk a mess of opened binders, pencils spilling from cases. Ana, he realized, had been digging through his things, looking for the pen.

George knew then that whatever intermittently drew them together, they were through once and for all. But he didn't know that he had just seen her for the last time.

After his guests filtered out (puzzled by the guest of honor's absence), he polished off a bottle of prosecco by himself. He sat in his empty apartment, glared at Ana's artwork and the general chaos of plastic cups and crumpled napkins, discarded husks of the evening's merriment.

George didn't even learn of Ana's death until about a week after the fact, when a friend called to offer her condolences. "I know you two were close," she said.

George's inner gallery of Ana-memories pestered him with fragments of her. Ana on his couch, ash tray balanced on her stomach while she complained about lazy friends selling more work than her. The way she couldn't pass a stray cat without trying to pet it or feed it something. Her love of flowers and inability to care for them—the vases of wilting daffodils in her studio.

George wished, perversely, that he could have written her obituary himself. A few splintered phrases lingered with him and surfaced sometimes: *Disaffected youth. Sarkis briefly attended Cooper Union but abandoned her studies. Cut off before achieving her full potential.*

A tragic accident. Swerved off the bridge late Tuesday night. The moonlit scene a tableau remarkably akin to the artist's own work…

And then she became an object, at last, of wonderstruck, glowing attention.

Nobody gave George any credit. Nobody remembered that he was the one who had found her in the first place.

A small eon later, it did not surprise George to find the glass pen stuffed between one of his filing cabinets and the wall. He told himself to throw it out. Or lock it away somewhere.

Instead, he watched the pen while it sat on his desk. Like he expected it to move or melt. It didn't. Light refracted through its handle and peppered the woodgrain.

George burrowed through books, students' papers, old articles (the thing for *Skiagraphia* about recent classicizing trends, her up-and-coming coterie), until he found them again: a set of cards covered with gold writing in his own hand.

He turned to one of Ana's pieces on his wall: a portrait of a young woman, her face half in shadow. A curved triangle of light disrupted the shading on her left cheek. She was seated beside a pool in a garden full of daffodils—and she was drawing something. George flipped through the cards until he found the right label:

A Narkissa, *2012*

> *Although the woman in this scene holds a sketchpad in her lap, her work remains deliberately unclear. Her feet descend below the water's surface, breaking the daffodils' reflections, so that they dissolve into unctuous, meaningless signs inscribed amid dissipating ripples. This sort of pseudo-script reflects Sarkis's ongoing interest in what art historian George Postman has termed "callimegraphs," that is, a kind of calligraphy that defies comprehension or readability, a visual nonsense language. The particle "me" (*μή *in Greek signifying "no" or*

"not") speaks to the illegibility of Sarkis's graphemes as well as the egocentric nature of her work, its "me"-ness.

A sound between a sigh and a hum filled George's chest. Something was wrong. He didn't know what, but he had to fix it.

He looked back at the pen, which remained where he had left it, on his desk. Still hadn't melted. George rummaged through his desk drawers for one of her old inkwells.

He had to wait a moment for the tremors running through his fingers to fade. Then he edited his own writing. He added a new sentence to his old description: *However, in spite of Sarkis's insistence that her calligraphy ought not to be read for any kind of recognizable meaning, four letters are in fact often identifiable amid her pen flourishes: A, S, G, P.*

That had been an old way of teasing her. He used to claim that he could see her signature floating through her ink. That it all signified something, whether she meant it to or not.

As he turned back to the drawing on the wall, George convinced himself that it had indeed changed. The woman by the pool was tracing a letter P on her sketchpad—in imitation, maybe, of a wobble of yellow lettering that spilled across the water out of a daffodil's reflection.

It felt almost like a greeting—Ana reaching out to him. George's blood climbed up from his heart and a vein below his jaw fluttered. He started a new label.

A Narkissa*, 2012*

In this piece, Postman and Sarkis's insights combine, and her callimegraphs turn into calligraphy of a more traditional sort. Postman's understanding of Sarkis's visual motifs imposes a kind of legibility upon the ordinarily illegible scene.

George hesitated, then added another line: *A coil of hair on the depicted woman's brow curls around itself, as though to represent the solipsistic spiral of her thought externalized.*

He watched the drawing.

Nothing happened. Maybe he hadn't seen right in the first place. Maybe he was imagining things, willing power into a pen overladen with memory.

The next morning, George woke to opalescent strands of light wavering across his walls, as though refracted through water. He crept through the apartment, chased the glow's source. The floorboards groaned, and not beneath his own footfalls.

And then—there she was. He found Ana.

George breathed her name.

But something was wrong. A weird shape glowed on her cheek, heedless of the unlit apartment. It took George a moment to figure out where that came from. At first he thought, oh hell, she's a ghost. But no—that wasn't it. He remembered the light and shadow that divided the face of the woman in *A Narkissa*, her cheek illuminated by the brilliant water beneath her.

The woman before him had bangs that curled a little above her brow; one lock spiraled into itself like a letter G.

"What's going on," whispered George, his voice hoarse.

"What's it look like?" she said with a shrug. "I'm back."

She stood in silence while George circled her, reassuring himself he hadn't dreamed her up. The reassurance wouldn't come. Perhaps he had dreamed her up. Did it matter? She was here. He could see and touch her.

"Where have you been?" he asked. "They said you drowned."

She shrugged noncommittally, just like Ana would have, and didn't answer him.

Ekphrasis

"Did you know you have admirers now? People are fascinated by you," said George. "They say you disappeared into your work on purpose. There's this one curator who swears she's caught glimpses of you, sometimes, swimming through different versions of *Echoes of Sea Sounds*. She's nicknamed it *Haunted Echoes*."

"That's silly," said the Ana-esque creature. "Why would I do something like that?"

Why would she reduce herself to a haunting? "I don't know," said George. He remembered her hiding behind her headphones while she sketched. How she craved and hated attention. He needed a new word for the weird jealousy he used to feel, of Ana's relationship with herself—the way she'd sink into her own head and leave him struggling to follow her, to find her.

The Ana-esque creature glowed, and George led her to the couch, where he touched the tattoo of light on her cheek, then laid a hand atop hers, thrilled by the blood, the heat in her veins. He lowered his head into her lap and felt her settle a palm across the back of his neck. Comforting him. He had a catlike urge to purr with delight.

He called a friend he'd promised to meet for dinner and lied to her, said he couldn't make it after all. He felt ill.

The Ana-esque creature slept too late, just like Ana, and stared out the window while listening to music, and she somehow managed to kill George's plants when he wasn't looking—or at least he joked as much, blamed her when his orchids withered.

She got moody, then, disturbed by his accusations—then gasped around a drowning kind of laughter when George held and kissed her.

All of that felt right.

Still, the Ana-esque creature remained just that: -esque, creature. Qualified, not fully Ana.

Perhaps her listlessness was too much, a caricature of Ana's. George tried to remember what would have made Ana happy (or less withdrawn), and so he urged her to work, littered pens and pencils and blank paper throughout the apartment. But she ignored them, the way the real Ana used to ignore— he didn't know what. Spectator sports. The crime shows he'd leave on while he cooked.

Sometimes he asked her directly: "Wouldn't you like to draw today?" But she always shrugged and said, "Don't really feel like it."

An Interview with the Artist, 2015

Q: Could you say why you're so uninterested in encoding readable meaning into your calligraphy? I'm sorry, callimegraphy, *I ought to say.*

A: You can just call it calligraphy if you want. Anyway—"readable meaning"? I think my calligraphy is readable. It's true I'm not spelling out signs you can read and hear in your head like words on a page, but it still means something—sort of. I guess I mean it's loud.

Q: Loud?

A: Yeah. Like a conch full of sea sounds. The kind of sound you almost think you're imagining. Does that make sense?

Q: I think so. What about the role of memory in your work—could you talk about that? That seems tied to some of these questions about legibility—the relationship between personal, private memories versus public histories and myths.

A: You mean how I draw things that only make sense to me and a handful of high school friends, then get depressed when nobody else understands? [Laughs.]

Q: You've referred to depicting your experiences with these friends.

A: Yeah—kind of. We were all first-first generation kids, my parents from Lebanon, theirs from Russia, Poland, Cambodia, and we all felt a lot of pressure to get good grades and stuff, which they did, I didn't. In the meantime we smoked behind the bleachers, got little tattoos we'd hide behind our cuffs and hair. We made up a secret code, junior year. A mashup of our parents' languages—mostly our favorite curse words. Everyone else thought we were nuts, witches speaking in tongues. I loved that.

Q: Where are these friends now? What do they think of your artwork?

A: We stopped talking a long time ago. I had a couple of bad relationships that took up a lot of space in my head—I forgot to stay in touch with people I actually like. You know how it goes—stupid patterns.

George studied the rendition of *A Narkissa* on his desk and tried to remember what the ripples and highlights had looked like before he imagined the lettering into them. He had checked them all. Every version, every variant and reproduction he could find had metamorphosed.

He set the glass pen to paper, waiting for a description to come out—of the thing under Ana's control alone. Something that could help him get her right. But the memory and words stayed dammed up, wouldn't budge.

George put the pen down, shooed away the threat of a headache.

"George?"

He tried not to recoil.

The creature's face continued to glow in the dim, the triangle of light lingering absurdly on her cheek. And the curling hair on her brow—nothing like Ana's—leered at him. She came closer and touched George's shoulder, then her fingertips ran up his neck, sank into his hair, combed through the strands as though to draw the worry out of his head. "Everything okay?" she asked.

"Yes, yes," said George, shaking her off. "Everything's fine. I just need some space right now. I have work to do."

"Ah."

A pause.

And then, the creature said the worst thing possible, murmured it sweetly: "Dear sort-of-Pygmalion. She never loved you. You were supposed to help get her attention, a reputation. But you failed her, and that was when she started to leave you."

Some foul alchemy made George's blood into slush. He stared at his own hands, then turned to bite back—but the creature had left.

He told himself to get back to work, to fix this, and reached for the pen.

It wasn't there.

Even as he grabbed his bag, upturned it in desperation, fell on his knees to search beneath his desk, George knew he wouldn't find it.

And then the pigments of his memory shifted around.

Some pieces of the past glowed, their saturation painful, while others faded. Like a new curator had broken into his head to rearrange his history, and a gallery opened up at the front of his mind, full of Ana—no, full of the Ana-esque creature this time. Bright adoration flooded through George. Papery light. The weird radiance of her.

But then the light cut grooves into him—an icicle, a chisel carved and rewrote his inner pictures and thought.

He found the creature holding the pen.

Ekphrasis

She was writing across and around Ana's art on George's walls, inscribing and surrounding it with new words. A legible history. Just the ingredient George had always thought would help.

George resisted a distant urge to laugh. So. The creature couldn't draw, but she could write. Of course. She was George's creation, after all, and that was all he could do himself, all he could give her.

For a moment, admiration made George light-headed, as he followed the dance and swoop of her hand. This glimpse of Ana's old beauty, become comprehensible, was something he had always wanted, needed, so, so much.

His thought tangled in a web of writing and light. He saw hair and ripples become initials, a drowned woman's face, golden flowers, or were they stars?

And then he could no longer tell which thoughts and memories and wants were real and which were distortions, which were his and which were hers. He drowned in light and ink.

Ana Sarkis
American, 1987-2015
Echoes of Sea Sounds, *2015*
Graphite and ink on paper

> *In this homage to Romantic landscape painting, a solitary young lady (perhaps a stand-in for the artist herself) stares out at a turbulent sea as a storm gathers in the distance. Meanwhile, a man's silhouette floats upon a wave, his features half-obscured by sea foam. Bubbling letters in an uninterpretable alphabet seethe around him and consume him. The woman contained within the scene is simultaneously positioned as its subject and architect (in her clear capacity as artist-analogue). She holds one hand to her ear, as though to listen to the swirls of linework surrounding her.*

Five Poems

Marisca Pichette

Against cold stone

Queen, Queen,
on the floor.

      Lips parted & pursed
      Jaw tight & grinding

Tell me, standing
as I have never stood
breathing
as I have never breathed
ruling
as I have never

Where is the girl with the raven hair,
frostbitten skin & bleeding lips?

Where is the girl whose fingerprints
still smudge the edges of my glass?

Her heels left furrows in the dirt
dragged into a world she'd never seen
by men she feared
like thorns & ash.

Queen, Queen

Your muscles worn from tension
Heart wearied by anger

Where did you leave her, in those woods?

The woman who returned, blood on her hands
& not her lips,
feet scarred by winter—
was not the fairest.

She learned
there is nothing fair
when skin breaks
as willingly as glass.

I watch you
        watching me
watch your altered face—

& I almost see the girl
they dragged away
in the woman you dragged
back.

Thumbelina

It is said that a dying flame can come back
to life, if only the breath of a girl
is expended to keep the fire
going.

It is said that under even the deepest ocean
there lies another ocean,
brine like the tears
of virgins.

It is said that if you take out the heart of one,
scoop out her insides and lay them
on the table, glaring in the surgeon's lamps,
you can remove her son
while she lies dying.

It is said that she will float
or sink
and neither eventuality
will make him wrong.

It is said
that she can go anywhere
if she is not
alone.

It is said that Thumbelina
is small, weak, helpless
trapped in the softest breeze
cast by her last
breath.

For an eye

Mary, Mary,

third time's the charm—
or curse.

We asked you to
wake for us.

Claw your way up
from slumber

and bleed
to our pleasure.

Are you a monster? or does
the mirror show only

one
        ugly
face,

parasites huddled
along the bathroom floor.

I drip down the drain
whispering—

Mary, Mary,

That's not
my name.

Five Poems

women and

children children children
faceless, voiceless,
identified only by their innocence

women *and*
and them and them
and?

what are women without that "and,"
that connection to something
that needs protection

the children will grow will die
will make lives of their own
but the women remain

and
and
and.

what futures have we
bound to a mass of little limbs
always wanting, always asking

for care without authority
for love without reciprocity
for protection women have never been allowed

to give.

women and
women and
women wishing

for names so easily given
to children
until they grow into

women too.

Meditation on the contours of absence

and photograph,
a face in a frame built
of edges & angles
cruelly defined

she feared
      ink
dripping, soaking,
reflecting a shadow more clearly
than a face. Eyes
like & unlike Mouth
closed & gaping Ears
sticking out Hair
dirty.

She feared the borders of herself.

A picture slips from
mother-of-pearl braces
to cut the muse
      —unlucky mirror
of a diminished
face.

      —from Anne Carson

Winter Blues

Laura Cranehill

I SPEND ALL afternoon out by the fence. My knees get wet in the snow, and my breath condenses in my beard. There is clarity in mundane labor. I feel something like peace while working, though the peafowl are still rattled from the storm. They circle around me, confused, scrambling over the ice and stepping on each other's tails.

I pat the frozen ground near my shins, and nothing's there. I'm missing some nails.

When I look up, my breath catches in my throat. A girl is sitting on the fence a little way down. She's wearing spotted snow boots and a yellow sundress over her winter coat.

"That fence isn't too stable." My joints creak as I stand.

Smiling, she yanks on one of her braids. "It's holding me up just fine."

"Well, you can get off it, as far as I'm concerned. I don't want you getting hurt."

She itches her nose, then hops off.

The sun comes out and clumps of snow shake off the trees. The peacocks yelp as they run, their feathers like stained glass fracturing the cool light.

"Do you have any milk?" the girl asks as she walks up to me.

"Sure, I do."

She smiles sweetly, like she's been practicing those dimples. She grabs my hand and holds it as we walk to the house. Her fingers are so small compared to mine. Pink nail polish splotches a few of her fingernails. But only a few, as if in the middle of trying to look pretty, she found something better to do, and left it alone for another day.

In the kitchen, I pour a tall glass of milk. I only have one chair. I pull it out for her and pat the seat. When she climbs up onto it, she spreads her yellow skirt over her knees. Her chin barely comes over the tabletop.

"Here you are, honey." I put the glass down in front of her and rest my hand on the back of the chair.

She grabs it with both hands and takes a big, long gulp, smacks her lips, and says, "From a live cow! MMMM!"

That's when I take the shotgun leaning against the side of the fridge and shoot her in the spine.

She turns into a rabbit, twitching and kicking. I shoo her out of the house, guiding her with my foot. She hops along, one of her back legs jittering with annoyance. My muddy shoelaces trail along the laminate floor, which is supposed to look like wood but doesn't.

She sits there on the doorstep for a little while, fixated on the peafowl, her ears flickering like a fly keeps bothering her. The birds cock their heads to get a look back at her. Flustered, they show off and shake like chandeliers in a hurricane.

After a while, the rabbit stares at the kitchen window, where I'm watching. It makes me uneasy, so I back away.

I've got work to do anyway. Got to fix that fence.

I go to the garage to find nails. A broken fence is a chore you shouldn't be careless about, and one thing you shouldn't put off fixing. I can't afford to have the peafowl getting out, they are how I make my humble living. But the real reason you need to mend a fence right away isn't because of what can get out, it's about what can get in.

There's a burn mark on the garage door, about three feet wide and four feet tall. When I go into the garage, I can't guess why the fire could have started, or what could have stopped it. I stand over the drain in the middle of the concrete, trying not to inhale the stink of ammonia. A peacock scrambles on the roof.

When I open the first cardboard box I come to, the smell of old pine rises and fades into the musty air. It's mostly filled with Christmas wreaths, bent hangers, and my mom's wind chimes.

I sigh when I see the wind chimes, so dusty and tangled. I had taken them down after my mom left. She always kept them up because she said spirits can't resist ringing them. Every time they'd go off, far from any window, or air vents, or anything else that could cause a draft, she'd sing and laugh and clap her hands. My mom was comforted by the presence of ghosts.

When they chimed during the day, it was fine. But usually, it was the middle of the night when they'd really go at it, making a racket that echoed down the halls. It gave me the chills. That's why I unhooked them, tied them together, and put them in a box.

When my mom lived here, she sprinkled our home with stolen holy water and burned cedar chips in all the corners to keep bad spirits away. But the knowledge of the occult went with her, and ever since, winter has always been left to run of its own accord.

My chest squeezes a little. I don't want to think of my mother. Not right now. During summer, you can remember things like that. But not during the winter.

I close the box back up.

I have to go to the corner store again, even though I went yesterday, and the day before. I bag up all the aluminum cans I drank empty last night, and I haul them into the back of my Astro van.

My hands shake as I try to get the key in the ignition. I have a hard time in winter. The lack of vitamin D shuts my body down. My brain gets foggy, and I forget things. And with everything else that goes on, I need to keep my head as sharp as possible. It's tough, though. I can't help the way I am; it's in my blood. That's how my grandfather died. Killed himself, in the middle of winter, because something in his dreams told him he wasn't going to see the sun again. And if his last days were going to be winter days, he didn't want to live them.

But I have to fight that urge. No use in giving up. I try to get out of the house as much as I can, which means driving to the corner store nineteen miles away. There's nowhere else to go.

A lot of ice makes for a stressful ride, though. Driving down the road upsets the cans in the trash bag, and the noise rattles my nerves. I don't know anyone else who doesn't have a four-wheel drive, unless they're in the city, where the plowmen live like kings.

I can't remember the corner store man's name. More than a few times I've asked him, but that's not the sort of information I can hold in my head. And since I've seen him almost every day for years now, it's too late now to keep on asking.

He counts cans while I wait. Each can earns me a ten-cent deposit, which doesn't sound like much, but it adds up.

When he hands me the receipt, I joke, "Half my family is in the aluminum business." He laughs the same disinterested laugh, then puts the receipt down on the counter, even though he knows I'm going to hand it right back to him for the next batch.

Today, I have a worrisome time. I compare each 24-pack to the others, trying to find the one with the least-dented cardboard. I'm on edge as I listen for the little bell above the door that means it's opening. If someone else comes in, what do I do? Smile? Do I say hi? Should I pretend like I don't see them?

They're all so friendly around here, even if they don't really know each other. I can't figure out why, or how.

Today I get lucky and no one walks through the door. Probably everyone is staying in, fixing up after the storm. Besides that, the store has nails on clearance. They are a little beat up, the package is in poor condition, but they're usable. Maybe things are going to get better. Maybe that was the last storm of the season.

The next one that comes is a woman. Young, but still a woman—and good Lord is she good-looking. Her hair is curled, and she wears the littlest cut-off jean shorts, even though it's freezing outside. She's selling something. Vacuums, I think, and she sure is selling them hard. She wants to come in and show me how to work the thing. I let her, of course. Then I slit her throat with my hunting knife.

She turns into a white cat with a pink scar, like a second satisfied smile, spread beneath her jaw.

She wants to stay and curl up in my lap, but I hate cats. I interrupt her purring by grabbing the skin on the back of her neck. I march across my property and toss her beyond the fence.

The next morning when I make breakfast, one of the eggs I crack open has a partially formed chick in it. That's the problem with farm fresh eggs, I guess. And the problem with forgetting to gather them. I should take down that red light and just let the hens settle down and rest for the winter, like an animal is supposed to do. But I need protein in the winter. And, as the good book says, the good Lord put animals on this Earth to serve man.

I microwave a few strips of bacon instead and have to wash it down with thirty cents worth of can. As I eat, I try not to think of the bloody clot that flopped onto the pan, dripping with yolk, its wings just fleshy stumps, its eye open and blind.

The next thing I remember, it's dark. Either a snowstorm has come in without me noticing, or the night. It's hard for me to tell. There's a soft knocking at the door.

When I open it, an old woman stands there, smiling and wearing a dainty cross on a silver chain, clasping her hands together.

"Mom!" I respond with a cut-off gasp. There's an air bubble aching in my chest.

She laughs, too happy to think of something to say, and wraps me in a hug. Jumping up and down in my arms, she seems so tiny. Her familiar smell seeps softly into my nostrils. Dried corn, old flannel sheets, and burning cedar.

"Mom." My voice is muffled against her sweater.

"It's been so long!" She pushes me aside so she can come in. Her right hipbone pops whenever she steps on that leg. She's bent over, too, more than the last time I saw her.

"Oh my, oh my," she says, shaking her head as she looks around the kitchen. She notices the missing cupboard doors, the moist clutter, the peeling walls, the stench of a mildewed home that's been misused.

She makes a tsk, tsk noise with her tongue. It reminds me of when she used to call the peafowl over to eat. Her "kiss the cook" apron still hangs on its hook by the stove, so she pulls it down and ties it around her plump waist. She picks up some cheese stick wrappers lying on the table, sweeps the layers of crumbs from the counter into her cupped hand, and dumps it all into the overflowing trash can.

"It's been a long time, Ma. I have so much to tell you."

She doesn't glance up from her cleaning. "Oh, really?"

"I've done so much living that I wish you had been here for."

"Hmmm." There's a bald spot growing on the back of her head.

"Although right now I can't remember exactly when those times were, when I thought you would have been proud of me, or at least when you'd figure I turned out okay."

She laughs and cranks her head up and down, her stringy curls bouncing.

"Let me warm you up some milk, sweetie." She opens the fridge and sticks her head way far in, grabs the jug and lets the door close. "You always got tummy aches, and I'd make this before you went to bed."

"Yeah, I remember, Ma." What I don't say is that it had never really helped.

She pours a glass of milk in a coffee mug and puts it in the microwave and sets it for half a minute.

When she turns around, she doesn't blink, even though I'm pointing the shotgun right at her.

"Thanks for cleaning up some, Mom. I love you." I'm crying.

"I love you too, honey pea." She smiles gently back at me.

I can't very well shoot her in the face, so I aim at her chest.

The shot rings out, the jolt of the gun racks through my body as the bullet hits her.

Her head hangs forward and whimpers. A pool of blood soaks through her sweater. She totters, falls forward, her bent leg stopping her from crashing on the floor.

For a second, I stand there, my gun at my side, my pulse hammering, my hands numb.

Why hasn't she turned into anything? A mouse? A mink? A little songbird, maybe, with a voice like peeling wind chimes?

I run to her and put my hands on her shoulders. I take them away again, not sure how I should hold her. The leg keeping her from falling shakes, and she crumples.

That's not the way a body falls after it gets shot, I tell myself. Though, I wouldn't know.

She's not gone yet, though she doesn't seem to be completely here anymore, either. She's humming a tune. After a few off-key notes, I recognize it as a commercial jingle from the '80s.

The song falters, peters out. I tell her I love her again, but this time my voice quavers, like I'm not actually sure. As her breathing stops, I realize I'll be haunted with that, wondering if I sent my mother off to eternity while she wondered whether I really loved her.

There's the strange halo of her scraggly hair. The hand folded over her chest, blood between the fingers. Her eyes, only barely distorted by death.

I leave the house with her still in it. I can't stay in there anymore. I go out with my ax, the one I keep propped up against my front porch.

The fence is weak and breaks easily. First, I chop away the parts injured by the storm. Then the other places. Where I found the little girl. Where, one time, I found the blind man with the compound bow, the arrows littered on the ground sawed in half. Where I once found the boy with bruised hands. More and more and more, it all comes down.

My hands get cold, and the slam of the ax numbs them further. The wood splinters, the jagged nails exposed. I should be breathless, or tired, though I don't feel it. It's like I'm watching someone else's dream.

"Come get me, then!" I shout, my stomach twisting and sour as I wait to see what the woods will bring, squinting to find the shape of things in the dark. Eventually, my eyes clear up. I see the outline of the gnarled oaks, bare of leaves. The birch trees naked against the snow. And I see the devil.

He has the murky eyes of a woman and an oversized jaw. His neck is long and pulsing, his skin taut like a stretched bat wing. His lips are darkened with blood, his tongue reaching out from his mouth and tasting the falling snowflakes. Whatever they tell you of the devil, remember that he is a man of sensuality, and he is an angel of needs.

A man shouldn't have to confront this sort of darkness while he is alive. But take your complaints to God. I promise you, He won't give a damn. If He did, it wouldn't happen. The outcome of that ancient war is clear: God has won. His peon enemy couldn't even look at you if God didn't let him through the gate of the world. But he does. Take it all up with Him and see if he cares.

"What do you want?" My voice cracks, I'm already tired of yelling.

"Your filthy soul," he says. He sounds like anyone else. Your uncle, your neighbor. Your father, your son.

"I'm not guilty of anything. Except for not loving my fellow man." And possibly matricide.

"That's enough," says the devil. He has too many teeth in his grin, and the skin in his throat is so thin that I can see his pulse flickering under, large and erratic enough to say maybe it's not his pulse, but something else he's carrying inside him.

Moving toward the fence, he says again, "I want your filthy little soul." When he puts his hands on the broken wood, his hands flicker, as if he is just a shadow next to a sputtering candle.

I square my shoulders, plant my feet firmly on the ground.

"You can't have it." My voice is hoarse. "You can't have any of my property."

The shape of the devil expands, and it fills the forest and vibrates inside me. I can feel something in my throat, at that place where my pulse throbs when I am afraid, something swelling and moving like a pupil looking around inside me. *What doesn't belong to heaven, belongs to me.* I don't know if it's the devil's voice or my own.

With a deep, hurting breath, I reach back and heave my axe at him.

Nothing answers but the smack of the wood handle hitting bark, and then the muffled thud of metal dropping to the snow. And a lone peacock, awake for no reason, circling the house, and calling, he-elp, he-elp.

The wind picks up, a blast that could peel skin. I just stand there and let it bite through my body.

When I go inside, the screen door slams behind me.

Back in the kitchen, I nudge the thing that might have once been my mother, trying to wake her up.

She doesn't wake. I think of what to do with her.

The ground's too frozen to dig. I could cover her with snow, but if I did that, I would have to see her again once it warms up, and it wouldn't be a nice sight to see. If she's a real body, I mean.

The microwave beeps a reminder. Nobody's taken the milk out yet. I cross the kitchen and pop open the door. I grab the glass and sip. It's still warm.

I take it to bed with me. My tummy hurts.

I wake to the unusual quiet of morning. I carry out her body, but almost drop it when I notice that all the peacocks are dead.

I rage and yell—how did this happen? I did everything right. I protected my house, I protected my land. As is my right and privilege, and as is my duty.

There's some blood, but less than you might think. Dark like wild animal's blood, splattered up the side of the barn wall. Little trails of it here and there. Loose feathers snag in the shattered fence. But mostly, the birds don't have wounds. They're piled up in little heaps, necks broken. Like sacs of damaged silk, bright against the snow.

Shuffling through the massacre, I notice one peacock on the roof, bracing himself against the wind, icicles frozen to his chest. He's spooked, but still alive.

I coax him down, tsk tsk, and carry him into the house.

Winter Blues

We sit in the corner store parking lot, the peacock and me. He just eyes me, the long sapphire veil of his tail tucked between the seats.

At first, I was surprised he wasn't afraid of me. But I suppose he knows who's fed and sheltered him all his life. He stayed by my side when I took my mom out into the woods. I won't forget that he was with me through a thing like that.

He's scared of the great outdoors though. Which is understandable, after what he's been through. I let him stay in the house now. With his long tail, he couldn't turn around in the rooms very well, so I cleaned up some old storage boxes. Threw away some stuff I didn't need, brought out some things I had forgotten about but now was glad I had. I hadn't realized how much dust that old cardboard had been collecting until I carried it all to the side of the road. Got back in the house and felt like I could breathe better.

A tap on the passenger window, and both of us startle. I turn to see a woman with red mittens, snow flecking her hair. She's wearing this sweater that says, "Proud mother of pugs," and has an ugly little dog wearing a party hat made of sequins.

She waves, and I can hear her excited voice, but I can't make out her words.

I scramble for the keys and put them in the ignition. But then I glance up at her, and her smile. My finger hovers over the button that rolls down the window. Then I snatch it away and grip my knee. Clearing my throat, I gather my courage, put my finger back again, and press down.

"You have a little friend!" She says it in that high-pitched way people do when they're talking to animals.

The peacock stretches his neck as if he's going to peck her and see what she tastes like. But then he draws back and tilts his head up at her.

"I've seen you here before." She's looking at me now.

"I've seen you, too." I realize how that sounds, and my eyes dart around, trying to land on anything but her face.

"Are those wind chimes?"

Her eyes are nice. Brown and wide. Pretty, almost.

I look at the wind chimes where they are hanging from the rear-view mirror. "Yep."

"Oh, I love wind chimes. Have some on my front porch, and on the back." She leans through the window and into the car. Her clothes smell like maybe she put too much laundry soap in the washing machine.

The peacock jerks his head back, and forth and I figure he's about to dash over the back of the seat. I can't blame him. I'm leaning back myself, pressing away from her.

She taps the wind chimes and there's that distinct sound of cheap metal rattling against itself.

"Plink, plink!" she says.

I nod, don't know what to say.

"What fun." She finally pulls herself out of the car. "Well, it's nice to meet you. And your little friend." She snickers and wiggles her fingers at the peacock. "You're just about the only one who lives around here that I don't know. Next time you see me, be sure to say hi."

I nod again, embarrassed.

She turns around, and I release my breath. I didn't know I was holding it. Her sweater has red buttons down the back, in a weird place close to her spine. Useless buttons. But pretty, I guess.

She jerks back so she's facing me again. My eyes get wide, and I hope she can't tell by my face that I was thinking about her buttons.

She says, "Oh! I never asked you what your name was."

I scratch my beard. "It's Ben."

"What a lovely name. I'm Penny."

When she really leaves, I make fun of the peacock for liking her, but not too hard. I can remember what happened to him and his family. The guy's just lonely, that's all.

Winter Blues

I pop open a beer, and a few bubbles spew out and evaporate on the steering wheel. "In the summer, I'm going to order you some of the finest-looking peahens in the country. Five, all for you, buddy."

He squints his little eye at me.

"Naw," I say, "Make that ten!"

He can't wait for summer. Neither can I.

Il Mago

ART BY ISOTTA SANTINELLI

The Dance of Life
(After Edvard Munch)

Adam Lawrence

Look. Over there across the lake.
A yellow gazebo with terraced garden,
red flowers, green grass.
Men and women still
with the flush of youth
on their smiling faces.
Their buoyant figures dance
under a soft gauze light—
the artificial multi-hued glow
of motion picture props.

Certain details are easy to miss.
For example,
the shoreline behind you
is jagged with rocks like bleached bones.
The light has fallen, so you don't notice
the gazebo's gone,
the pretty flowers, too—just rotting
timber, weeds, organic compost.
You look into the face
of your dance partner
and see a loud laughing mouth, all teeth and tongue.

You've been warned,
so you stagger back from this
dress rehearsal run amok.

Is that you
on the left?

        Or on the right?

                (Or you're just
                out of frame,
                squinting, shading
                your eyes, waiting
                for the ferry—or
                something—to
                return.)

An Angel of God

Emma E. Murray

THE DAY AFTER St. John died, swaddled in my arms, was the day the airplane crashed in the valley. I'd just finished washing his tiny form in the basin and was getting his clothing ready while he lay wrapped in one of the good towels, his slack face drying under the cloudless sky. I had the onesie from Mamaw in my hands, smoothing it between my fingers and wondering how the sky could be so beautiful when the heavens should've been opening up to weep, when I saw something come sailing into the valley, just above the treetops and silent as a monk.

I had to shield my eyes. The soundless figure was a blip of white haloed by sunburst. My breath caught in my throat. I was sure it was an angel of God, but then it changed before my eyes. It became a plane, the small kind that rich folk like to show off in. I watched as it drifted down, a white whisper into the treetops, and disappeared into the foliage. The mountains echoed with the roar of limbs ripping from their trunks and a flurry of birds scattered into the air. Then all was quiet again, as if it hadn't happened at all.

For a while, I pretended like it hadn't. I dressed St. John in a clean cloth diaper and then the terrycloth blue onesie with a yellow duck embroidered on the chest. The last thing from Mamaw before she passed not long after I found out I was with child. I combed the wisps of fawn-brown hair on his two-month-old head and held him close to me, rocking him in my arms as I walked slow and deliberate to the grave I'd dug with my trowel and my own hands.

There was no reason to find a way into town for a funeral. Nobody was left to attend save myself. No reason for a plot in the churchyard with the family. That'd be too far for me to visit as often as I'd want to, so I knew I had to bury him down from the house, near the little creek. It was pretty there, shady and the ground was soft and mossy. Sure, the preacher wouldn't approve, but he's wrong about a lot of things. That's why I don't waste my time there anymore. No, this would be better. A comfortable place for his head to rest, under the earth but forever nearby; a little wooden cross to mark it with his name written as pretty as I could. The name I'd picked from my favorite book from school; a good and honest man's name who was also taken too young.

My hands shook as I set him down, but I couldn't bring myself to cover him. Not yet. His placid face, already darkening from that disrespectful, violent hand of death. No, I couldn't do it. I didn't say a word, but my heart prayed louder than my voice ever could. *Please God, give him back. I can't take it.* And that's when I heard the sound of the Lord calling me.

High-pitched, thin screeching, like when a frog or fish has the life squeezed out of them, but much louder and full of terror; it wasn't at all the glorious sound I'd expected from an angel, and yet I instinctively knew what it was. I couldn't leave St. John there, for fear some wild thing would carry him off, so I wrapped him in a blanket and set him in his cradle in the bedroom before hurrying out to follow the sound.

My heart throbbed against my breastbone as I stumbled through the tall grass and weaved between trees. I could feel my pulse behind my eyes, and my temples and 'round the nape of my neck ran with a cold sweat as if I was fevered. No pastor had ever preached about that, but I knew it was the angelic voice that caused it, along with the nausea and racing thoughts, flashing through my mind like secret messages written in light. Entranced, I followed the sound into the valley, where the plane had gone down.

It was easy enough to find once I got close. Though the canopy had enveloped it from above, below a trail of dangling branches and ruin led me along. The wings had been shorn from its sides as soon as it'd entered the forest. They lay in strange angles, tossed into the embrace of the trees. Farther down, I could make out the fuselage, unnaturally white among the dappled shadows. The otherworldly sound had dulled to an irritating hum, like a child's shriek muffled through a pillow.

I climbed through tangles of undergrowth to reach the wreckage and peer inside. My still healing womb ached with the exertion, but I continued on. Branches had snaked through the windshield and caught the pilot in their arms, winding through his open mouth and pinning him to the seat. A heavy headset threatened to slip off, trails of blood congealing down his face. His eyes were concealed by sunglasses, and I thanked the Lord in a hushed whisper that I did not have to witness their lifeless stare. That was when I realized the sound was not coming from inside the cockpit but farther into the forest. My mind was suddenly bombarded with images of torture and agony, and I knew I was close to finding the angel.

Slinking through the branches, crawling over logs while insects rose in anger and scurried across my hands, twigs catching in my hair and etching faint lines of blood across my face, I continued through the dense brush, thick and undisturbed by the airplane. I knew he was there ahead. I could hear the monstrous voice calling me, though it was weak. Then I saw the angel.

 His arms were stretched out between two trees, and he hung between them like Jesus on the cross. From his bowed head, beneath the blood-streaked mop of hair, his mouth gaped open and the terrible, inhuman sound still ushered forth, though cracking and weaker than ever. His lower half was missing, nowhere to be seen in the rubble around, and his intestines draped down in red ropes, waterfalling to the forest floor. Behind him, beams of sunlight peeked through the trees and backlit him in holy light.

He didn't look like I'd expected based on all the sermons, Christmas cards, and illustrated bibles I'd seen, but still I knew he was an angel. The moment I saw him, a voice like a thousand voices boomed in my mind and told me, through the voice of the Lord, that this horrid creature was sent just for me.

His eyes were closed, and he didn't seem to notice when I approached, though I wondered if perhaps he was too deep in prayer, communing with God about what would happen next. It occurred to me that angels often appeared as a sort of test, making sure you were worthy of the miracles they came to bestow, so I set to work immediately on freeing him. Careful hands dislodged the tangled intestines from the bushes before lifting him from his perch, climbing back down to carry him home. It was difficult to carry him, though he was not as heavy as I'd expected. I never realized how much weight our legs held. Still, my shirt was soaked with sweat by the time the house came into view.

The angel still hadn't opened his eyes, but I felt his ragged breath against my chest while I carried him, though I was relieved his terrible noise stopped as soon as I had removed him. Laying him across the kitchen table, carefully coiling his innards into a neat bunch and placing them beneath him, I set to work straight away. I wrung warm water out of clean cloths, using the good towels even knowing they'd be ruined. I'm no nurse, but I knew I had to keep everything from drying up. I wrapped his waist in plastic wrap, carefully pressing the wet towels around him first, and waited. He remained silent save some wheezing through the first couple hours and the first time I changed out the wound dressing.

I felt strange in my house with two heavenly, muted bodies. A heaviness grew on my shoulders, and I fiddled with my hands, unsure of how to keep from being idle. I washed the used towels and hung them to dry, hoping it'd happen quickly in the breeze so that I'd have them ready again for the next cleaning. As I was wiping down the sink, wringing the red, tainted water from the rag before wetting it again, I heard a gasp behind me. My whole body shuddered as the wincing, high-pitched screech that had brought me to the angel rang from him again, though quieted to a near whisper by his strained throat.

I wheeled around, grasping the sink behind me as my legs weakened under his haunted stare. He seemed to look through me to another plane, yet still I pushed through my fear and forced him to lock eyes with me. I knew it worked because my mind seemed to fuse with his in a sudden flash of white light and warmth. I cried out in the brief moment of ecstasy, but he looked frightened and confused, and I realized he might still be testing me, so I composed myself.

His lip quivered as he tried to speak, but only fragmented sounds escaped in the same hoarse squeaks as before. His eyes roved my face, searching for comprehension, and I wondered if he was speaking a celestial language I couldn't understand.

"Shh, there, there. I'm taking care of you. Here, drink some water." I offered the cup I'd readied to his lips, but he took only the smallest sip before gagging and turning his head away. "Tell me what you need, and I'll fetch it. I want to help you." Then it was my turn to tremble as I leaned closer, feeling his breath hot on my face as I whispered in his ear, "Tell me what I need to do so you'll bring him back."

His mouth continued to move in shapes as if he were speaking, but there was nothing except the noise. I turned my head, nearly pressing my ear against his lips, trying to make any sense of his labored sounds. Then I heard something resembling words, like a whisper through static. I closed my eyes and forced them into real words, teasing out his command until my mind flooded with the image of a stained-glass window I'd seen as a child, depicting an angel with wings outstretched against a blue sky.

"A stained glass? But I don't know how." I looked at him, pleading with my eyes, but he only stared back in the same distant way.

I fell to my knees and threw back my head, my neck long and craning as I prayed for guidance. The orange-red rays of sunset sprayed through the kitchen window and fell across the angel, bathing him in light. I understood. God revels in the creations of man because it is through him it is created.

After fitting the bed with sheets and tucking him in to rest, I quickly gathered every glass and bottle in the house, laid them on the kitchen floor covered by the spare sheet and hammered them into broken pieces. Green olive oil and wine bottles, brown beer bottles, the yellow sunflower that decorated Mamaw's old wind chime, and the cobalt blue glassware that had been an early wedding present before Samuel ran off, I took them all and smashed them into puzzle pieces to be assembled. I knew I couldn't craft a stained glass with no practice or skill, not like the angel I'd seen in the chapel, but I tried a different approach with the materials I had.

The cement mixture slopped in the white bucket as I stirred it in the early evening twilight, the stars just beginning to speckle the sky and a light rain misting down. I poured it into the makeshift mold I'd sawed and pieced together, stomping the pieces of plywood into the mud until they stuck in the shape I'd envisioned. Then I scrambled to arrange the glittering pieces into something beautiful. An angel.

I rushed into the house once more, feeling the burning of the Holy Spirit flowing through my veins, and scrambled to find more of my most precious and beautiful objects to add to the artwork. The small white shells from when I visited the ocean as a child, the mother-of-pearl buttons I'd been saving for my favorite sweater, the red glass earrings and the fake diamond ring that had sparkled in the sun when I showed it off and lied that it was real. I added these all, sliding them into the thickening mixture, arranging them in neat lines and geometric patterns that radiated out through the angel's wings. By the time I finished, the rain had stopped, and the cement had hardened too much to change anything, so I forced myself away to go change the real angel's dressings, telling myself it'd look better when it could sparkle in the morning light. Not just a collage of trash, but something worthy of the Lord.

However, I couldn't sleep a wink, and just lay on the floor, one hand in the cradle on my son's chest, listening to the quiet breathing of the angel above us on the bed. When the first rays of sun fell through the cold morning air, I ran outside to see my masterpiece. It wasn't beautiful at all. A monstrosity, childlike and embarrassing. But wouldn't the Lord see my effort, and knowing my limitations, see the beauty in what I was able to create with my own humble hands?

The morning glowed as the sun rose over the mountains, but there was a stale stagnation, barren and foul, in the air. Perhaps it wasn't enough. I knew the angel would be disappointed before I even entered the room, but when I saw his far-off look, his breath shallow and his brows forced together in a tight frown, I wept. I fell from his side and crawled across the floor to the cradle where St. John lay, his skin more mottled and his face barely recognizable as my little sunshine.

Above us, I could hear a sputter and then a low moaning. I pulled myself back to my feet and stood at the foot of the bed. I noticed blood and fluids seeping through the towels and plastic wrap, puddling around him, and soaking into the sheets and mattress. His face was blanched, and I thought about all the blood he'd lost from the injury and subsequent wound dressings, but could an angel die? I bit my lip.

I gathered the angel in the blanket and into my arms, cradling his half-body like an infant as I carried him through the house and into the front yard to behold my offering. He instinctively clung to me with the little strength he had left, arm draped over my shoulder, and I noticed he was much cooler than before, almost cold to the touch. As we stepped into the orange morning, my eye caught two planes circling the valley like vultures.

I had to coax him to open his eyes, parting in a squint from the rising sun and scanning briefly across my sparkling masterpiece before closing again. There was no change in expression or evidence he'd seen what I'd worked so hard on all night. Something inside me dropped like a weight in my stomach, and anger churned in the burning bile, but wrath is a sin, and I knew the Lord was still testing me. Gently, I brought the angel back inside, nestled him into the quilts on the bed, and forced a dribble of water into his mouth with an eyedropper along with some baby Tylenol, even though I knew it wouldn't help much.

"Please, I tried my best. I really did. Now, help me. That's why you came, isn't it?" The words were scarcely a whisper in my dry, tight throat as I watched the angel's eyelids flutter, but he didn't answer. I clutched my hands into fists against my thighs. Swallowing the sob building in my throat, I threw myself across the room to my baby's cradle and tore his tiny, cold form from it, holding him against my chest.

I swung my body back toward the deformed creature on my bed and scowled, my lip rising high and my mouth bitter with venom.

"Are you what I get after all these years of prayer, faith, and absolute devotion? Where's my miracle? Look at my son. You asked for art, and I made it. I passed your test. I did everything I was supposed to my whole life. Now bring him back!" The words gushed out along with streams of tears and mucus. I fell to my knees, gasping for air between heaving sobs. "I'm sorry. I'm so sorry. Just, please, look at him. Please."

On my knees, baby still pressed to my bosom with one arm, the other hand raked across the sheet, clawing toward the angel. "He's more beautiful than anything else I could ever make. I'm no artist, but I'm a mother. That's what you made me, Lord. Give him back. Please, just once. Just this once."

The words disintegrated into guttural sounds and wheezes, but the angel turned his head and opened his eyes. I knew he saw my son: his discolored skin, his distending belly, his still chest. A fly landed on his face and tried to enter his nose, but I waved it away, holding back a curse. He saw that death was eating away at him and soon there wouldn't be enough to come back. Lazarus was empty four days, and my little St. John had already been gone for nearly three. My eyes pleaded with the angel; my every breath begged him.

He craned back his neck and fully opened his eyes, and when I followed his eyeline, there was the small painting hung over my bed of Jesus on the cross. Something inside me clicked, and I knew this was a sign.

I took St. John out to the barn first, swaddled in his bassinet, which I placed in the corner after sweeping away the straw. As I walked back to the house, tires crunched along the gravel road and men's voices drifted up in fragmented echoes from the valley. My blood raced through my veins, spurring me to hurry with my work.

The broken angel was hardly human at all by this point, having morphed in his dying into his true, strange, and unearthly appearance. His skin a translucent pale like a cave salamander, the blue of his circulatory system showing as if through frosted glass. The plastic wrap holding his guts in place had yellowed with fluid and pus, hanging loose and soggy, and the pink of his intestines peeked through, threatening to burst forth. His breathing was so slight as to only be perceived by a hand close to his nose to feel the faintest puff of air, no longer rabbit-like but slowed as if he were holding his breath to conceal the glimmer of life still within. When I picked him up in my arms, I could feel beneath the cool flesh something like the flicker of a flame.

As I walked him to the barn, I could see movement in the trees of the valley and more voices. I knew I had to work quickly. I laid him on a bed of straw while I tugged and dislodged the long, thin beams of the wall with a hammer. The roof groaned in protest to its shifting weight. I fashioned the cross on the floor, and then I dragged the angel's temporary body to its final position, his limp arms easy to manipulate and his head lolling back and forth only a moment before resting his chin against his chest. Light flooded my mind with every blink, incorporeal bells rang in incessant, painful reverberations, and a frantic energy crescendoed inside me. I needed to make a sacrifice of my own.

I took the knife and forced it through the left palm, and then struggling to do the same to the right while blood pumped hot and slippery from the wound. All around his body, I dripped and splattered blood before bending down to smear crosses in each cardinal direction. When I stepped back, it was already more achingly beautiful than I would've expected; my pain painting it more vibrant than even the doors of Passover.

I tore the soiled wrappings from his body and watched his intestines unfurl in pale coils around him. Flies had already begun to gather, and I swatted them away from his face and wounds as I carefully arranged the tendrils of flesh into the illusion of draping wings behind him. It was glorious to behold, and I could feel the overwhelming warmth of God building inside the barn. I knew it was time for the final touch.

Gathering straw around the foot of the cross, I had only to send one small spark from the lighter and all went orange with flame. The angel didn't move as his form caught fire. Thick, black smoke bellowed out around him, and I watched the angel transform into its true blazing form of God's love before scrambling to drag the bassinet out the barn door.

Behind me, I heard the footfalls of people running and their shouts. I didn't look. Instead, my eyes were on the angel, already darkening into the ash masterpiece I'd designed. They were asking about the smoke, the plane, crying out in despair and confusion, but my eyes had moved to my son. Trembling hands grabbed at my open jaw, tears running down my cheeks.

"He's breathing," I whispered, drowned out by their terrible chorus around me. "Praise the Lord! Look! His chest is moving!"

Tonight, the Moon is not Quite Complete

SJ Townend

It had been her, and if not her, then the spit of her: hair of titian waves, skin lit as if by moonlight, Celtic emeralds for eyes. *No, it couldn't have been her,* he thinks, and tries to return his focus to the theremin wand in the space between his hands, *as that would be impossible, impossible.*

Tonight, now, it is his gig, his time, his chance to shine from his up-lit spot on the stage in an otherwise dark hall. But now he's seen her, this woman who is like her but not quite like her, all he can think about is finishing his performance, stepping down into the crowd, and searching.

This same game of cat and mouse continues, month in, month out, as if he and her are trapped in a repeating loop of unrequited searching, a nightmare. But even though he wants to, he can't step down into the crowd now, he must perform.

A hundred faces are staring up at him, a hundred faces he cares not for, but a hundred faces who have paid money, good money, a large part of which, he hopes, will become his. He needs this money to pay his way if he survives the morrow.

The theremin, all polished steel and electromagnetic fields, beckons back his nimble hands. He makes wings, lifts his arms either side of his machine, and does as he has done before, does what he is good at, the one thing he is sure he is good at. He carves the air with his hands, chops the air up into shapes, sculpts her cheeks, her patrician nose, the chin, the face of his long-dead mother out of nothing but drunk-thick air. With the movement of his hands, corresponding sounds are heard, as he throws the contours of her face out into the ether.

The song of his mother's face is the melody they have all come for. It is the tune they've all heard before, the song that makes him able to attract such a crowd. *An overnight internet sensation,* they said, *you simply must see him play in the flesh, there is nothing quite like it. Such a sound from something never touched.*

Each part of her face is construed into sliding semibreves and minims. Each part of her face hangs, out of sight, in the air, and then dissipates, disintegrates, as if it were not there, and it was not really there, not in the physical world anyway. Some say he has magician's fingers which undulate, releasing a little magic into the world, and with wizarding hands, he depicts with his thumbs, her brows.

He continues to play the face of his mother, the shape of the face of the mother he remembers, as his eyes continue their quest in searching for her in the crowd.

Left hand oscillating back and forth, right hand descending, he shapes the waves of her hair, crimps the invisible gaseous molecules and motes of dust held up within, and each curl brings an eerie tone through the speakers on either side of him on the stage. In his mind, a tear rolls down her cheek. He paints it in the space in front of him with his index finger and lets the speakers cry out with depression.

The audience is taken with this emotion, their hearts throb harder with the beauty of the sound. And then, with a flick of his wrists, he is shaping his mother's almond eyes, twilling out each long dark lash with his fingertips, and the crowd are lifted from the sad place he had placed them in as the key of the oscillations change from minor to major. Resonating reverberations. Both melancholia and joy become entwined. His hands play on. Music from the electromagnetic whine of the theremin sprinkles an acoustic, near-sentient gift, like dappled sunlight through a forest canopy, onto and over the crowd.

The hundred nondescript faces are brought to tears, but he wants his set to be over, for it to be finished, because he wants to find her this time: the visitor who never stays. He wishes to follow her off into the night and cup her face in his hands and ask her who she is, this woman who is but is not quite his mother.

Will it be like all the other times she has come to watch him perform, close, but no cigar? More than likely. But he is desperate and from his accumulation of hopelessness, he manages to sift free a glimmer of hope.

There she goes again. He sees her, sees the light and dark of her long curls. She moves, skirts from location to location, pocket to pocket, a human-shaped firefly dancing amongst the crowd. Each time he spots her in the audience, she flits. *Is it her?* How can it be—his mother died thirty years ago.

He stares into the crowd once more and sees the faces of all those who are not her, not this entrancing apparition of familiarity, and watches the strangers he cares nothing for sway like willows in a spring breeze. They move in unison, under the control of the sounds he orchestrates all-the-while, while searching, searching. *No, no,* he thinks, *I am certain now, she is not there. Not anymore.* And the sadness this brings to his soul drifts like weightless ghosts into his music.

He plays his next song, from his solo space up on the stage. He is the closing act, the headliner, although he has never understood why people come. Just a man, a man who drinks; a single, aging man with a theremin.

He feels the sounds he generates are the sounds one might manifest if one were in a place without any sound at all, if one were caged alone in silence for an eternity. From nowhere, one might begin to hear a theremin wail. And it would make one feel more alone, he believes. He finds the sound haunting, the last sound he would wish to hear if he were alone.

And he is alone in a way, always has been since his parents died many years ago.

His father.

On the morning of Pa's thirty-seventh, something red opened up inside of Pa. Pa collapsed and died, no warning. He, then a boy, had found his mother, a shade of ash, down on the kitchen floor, furled over Pa's warm corpse.

His mother.

She too died truly that day, but trudged through two more years, tending and caring for the boy, now a man, until she chose to release her feelings, by opening up her wrists, on the morning of her thirty-seventh.

The man who makes the music now, then a boy, was left to be raised by strangers. He is now thirty-six. He is certain, knows, he will not make thirty-seven, he feels it in his chest, more so this night, with his birthday in the morn. He has daily tried to numb the pressure, the beginnings of problems, pains, with alcohol. Tries to take the edges off the beginnings of his end.

But he does not want to die, not yet, although he supposes he does not have a lot to live for, although this may be the thoughts of the writer, scribing this poor man's tale, inflicting on fictional characters their own inner fears and concerns. Such is the way. So much is hidden in literature and so much is hidden in music, between the shapes the words and notes make.

He is sure he will not wake tomorrow morning, the first day of his own thirty-seventh year, as both his parents were lost on the morning of their thirty-seventh—some things are written in the stars, cast there in unreadable symbols.

In a matter of hours, he will fall asleep and not wake up, something red, or black perhaps, will open inside of him, something beyond his control. And nothing feels in his control: the rise and the fall of the tides, the pain he feels building within his heart, the ever-increasing rent on his beach side property, whether she comes and watches him perform, whether she—this woman who is the carbon copy of his mother but then again not—stays until the end this night or leaves part way through. Nothing is in his control except for the sounds his hands release as they mark out the faces of the dead in the air around the theremin.

This, he can control.

He must play on, it is all he knows, and he has bills to pay. His beach house does not come cheap, and he craves the desolation of his abode, could not bear to live in shared accommodation with others, would miss the solitude of the horizon, the unabated company of gulls, the occasional basking seal. People, they do not tolerate the ways of a drunken artist.

So each month, he plays at the clubhouse in the bay along from the bay in which his house that opens up to the sea is on, and shapes out the face of his father, then his mother, and the crowd embraces the music. Sometimes he'll open up to requests, if energized by a new moon: the audience will hold up photographs, pass them to the stage, of people they have lost, people they wish to be considered, and he will take one or two of these images and sculpt songs for them with the air between his fingers and palms. *It is as if they are there,* they say, *for the briefest of moments.*

And what good does it do, he thinks.

"I cannot return, so tonight will be my last performance as I don't have much time left," he says each time before he performs, as he clutches his hand to his expectant, anxious chest, and the manager, each time, replies: "You will return, this is your reason, to perform, you have all the time in the world. The voice you bring, it is the voice of all souls gone, lost to a fog, crying as if they do not know how to return."

He plays his last song, a request from a man a little older than himself who had passed him a photo of a child. With his melody, more angelic than a well-played harp, he brings the grieving father, the entire audience to tears, enough tears to make an ocean of the floor, and it is a deep enough ocean to fully lose the woman he is searching for in the crowd to as he performs.

She has gone.

The crowd depart and he is left alone. He drifts backstage as bar staff and security clear up the venue, where he plans to collect his things. He tries to warm himself with more whisky and some positive thoughts, *she came to see my final performance,* he thinks, but it does nothing but sadden him furthermore, because she, as usual, did not stay.

He contemplates his lonely walk home, possibly his last walk home on the eve of his thirty-seventh, back to the house on the beach, how he will pour a thick glass of whisky, toast once more to all he has lost to the waves, to the knife-gray ocean, to whatever is left of the moon. The sea, vast and inexhaustible, is a stable in his life, perhaps the only rock, other than his whisky.

As he tidies away equipment, places cables and parts back into their correct housing, he catches a curl of brine scent in the atmosphere, which makes him crave hard the salt of ocean air. He needs to be near water. He makes one last trip to the gents before starting on the path home, which he will light with a torch although he knows the route like the back of his hand and finds a strange safety in the blanket that the isolation and the darkness provide.

Back across the stage, through the empty space which was packed to the rafters just half an hour earlier, through the door at the back of the room, he travels to the sink. Washes first his hands, bends forward, over the sink in front of the mirror to splash cool, cool water on his face. Still, the smell of the ocean. He is alone in the bathroom, the only sound, now the patrons have all left, is the rising gurgle of the drain. It is a hard balance to find: a place between intoxication and sobriety, a state of mid-ground necessary for the short walk home to be smooth. *Cool water helps,* he thinks. He straightens his spine, feels the click of each vertebrae slotting back into some resemblance of its place as he does so, and sees his tired self in the mirror.

And her.

She is behind him. Soft almond eyes, hair a little longer than he remembers his mother's hair, skin a few shades out, but cheekbones, jaw, lips he feels he knows, had once known. It's as if, he thinks, a selection of his mother's genetic traits have been distorted, blended, undone and reformed, to create something similar, alive, but not quite right.

Familiarity, yet this woman who visits often when he plays here is her and not her. Something more than her. He feels recognition, an attraction, and a simultaneous sense of repulsion.

Heart thumping hard, he clutches his palm against his chest again, fearful. *This is it. This pumppump will be my last.*

He turns. Of course, the lady in the mirror is no longer there, was she ever? He closes his eyes, rubs them, opens them again.

She is back.

"May I come home with you?" she asks, and he feels as if she has unzipped something, as if something has come undone in his mind, something he is both happy to entertain and also unhappy to sustain.

Slowly, he nods his head.

If this is how the fabric of reality is to unzip, so be it, he thinks, *and I have more than enough whisky for two at home.*

And this cannot be Mother, he thinks, *because she looks no older than me, and if it were mother, she'd look far older than me. There would be white hair, lines deep enough for one to fully lose ones' sane self within. I have not lost it yet, have not tumbled all the way down the hole. She is just familiar.* He tries to reassure himself: *she is just familiar, not family.*

A large whisky, measured in thumbs and fingers, three of those.

He shows her around his small home, apologizes for the mess, "hadn't been expecting visitors." Has he ever had visitors? She nods, smiles, and then she speaks. There is a sweetness to her voice reminiscent of childhood lullabies, but it is not the voice he remembers his mother having. *There is overlap,* he thinks, *it is as if this woman is a tracing, a silhouette of something cherished and long gone.*

"May I stay over?" she asks, and he is taken somewhat aback. He starts to rummage in the chest against the wall for blankets, soft bedding, so he can prepare a warm nest for himself in the living room, a room in which little true living has graced his time in the property. He is not dead though, not yet—his body is still warm to touch, unlike hers, which he notices is icy, when she places the palm of her hand on the side of his face and looks him in the eye and thanks him with sincerity for accommodating a stranger.

This woman, this woman who is but is not someone he recognises, she is as much a stranger to him he supposes as a stranger one might pass by on the street. Yet also, she feels like home. And in all of his homes, he has always slept with a knife underneath his pillow.

"Yes," he says, "you may have my bed." And she smiles with a smile he imagines could only be compared to the Mona Lisa or perhaps the mother of Jesus and, *is that a celestial halo rising behind her skull as she smiles,* he wonders.

"It's okay, child," she says, although she looks no older than him, younger maybe. "You may rest by my side, share the bed with me."

He nods, he likes the way her hand feels on his cheek, it is not a sexual feeling. He senses there is nothing expected, nothing to fear. Not yet.

It is late, but he feels restless, must be a better host, so he passes her his warmest sheepskin jacket to keep out the bite of the near-midnight air, and leads her down to the beach, says the whisky tastes sweeter there.

She follows, they kick off shoes, feel sand between their toes. He is not one for small talk, what purpose is there in talking about the weather, when one is stood underneath the beauty of the stars, the night sky, drunk beside the sea? *Nature says it all,* he thinks. So instead of small talk, he talks about his work—he worries the silence feels unnerving.

"The theremin," he tells her, with his tongue in his cheek and just an inch of whisky left in his bottle, "was used at the turn of the millennia by scientists to send music deep into space, in a concert for extra-terrestrials, an interstellar radio message."

She smiles, although he can't see her clearly with the beach only lit by the light of the moon and his old gas lamp. "I know," she says and points to the moon, waxing gibbous, "I know many things, and nothing is as it seems, and what a façade to make so much effort exploring the outer limits when so little is known about what goes on inside and within. The desert, the rainforest, the hadal zone, one's own mind and soul—none of these places yet have been fully explored."

He is muddled by this or believes it may be the whisky doing the muddling, as does the writer, portraying the events which are about to occur. He ponders as she continues to point at the moon. They are silent for a moment. They both stare up at the sky. The relentless crashing of wave up on wave, a cycle slowly moving forward, slowly moving back, is cleansing and also deafening.

"I'm not sure what you mean," he says eventually, his words almost lost within the pattern of the water pummelling the shore. He speaks so quietly he is not even sure he has spoken so repeats himself just to be sure. Aloud, his own words sound alien.

"The moon, for example," she says, and returns her finger to the sky, "is here and also here." Her arm drops, her finger now points to the white, rippling disc, the moon's partner, its reflection on the shifting skin of the sea. He thinks of earlier, the reflection of this woman in the mirror, how one was a copy of the other, one real, one not, and neither were his mother.

"The moon," she continues, "is not what it seems."

He knocks back the last of his drink. The alcohol burn does nothing to help him understand her words.

"You see it as a celestial body, a sphere of rock, orbiting another sphere of rock, shining back old light from a distant sun, controlling the ebb and flow of the tide," and he is not sure if she is making a statement or asking a question, or if she'll still be here in the morning, "but it is in fact a hole."

She leads him back to the house.

Will there be two sets of footprints in the sand come morning, he thinks, and she answers him, "Yes, yes, my child." But he is sure this time that he had not said this aloud, and he thinks of the painting his mother had hung on the wall in her bedroom, a gift from an overbearing god-botherer shortly after his father passed.

An image. Two sets of prints in the sand. Then one set of prints in the sand, and a message of hope, about how sometimes, when it appears that one set of prints has disappeared, it is not because someone has been deserted but because someone is being carried.

And he knows this memory should make him feel better, but it has quite the opposite effect.

He pours another drink for himself, offers her a top-up, which she declines, and she pats the side of the sofa. He slops down at her side. "Tell me," she says to the drunken man, "why drink so?"

He does not have a clear-cut answer, does not have a sharp mind, has not ever thought why, but only how and when, but he knows the answers is somewhere hidden in his childhood, his loss, grief, the sensation he won't make it past thirty-six, may not wake in the morning to see any footprints in the sand.

He tells her of his fear, his curse: he will not make it through to his thirty-seventh year, *it is written in his stars,* and she is silent for a moment.

"You say this is a given," she speaks eventually, "but not everything is as it seems." And she lowers the top of her shirt, reveals the skin above her breasts, and asks him to lay on his hand. "Go ahead, close your eyes," and he does so. His hand finds its place, he closes his tired eyes, and this is when he feels it.

He is taken aback at the power of what his mind's eye reveals. The lady continues to speak.

"You say your certain demise is written in the stars, there is a use by date stamped on your breathing corpse, well," she says, and he pulls his hand away as if he had scalded himself on a hot stove, "I have infinity etched into my soul."

Too much.

He does not remember after this. He falls asleep, and while he is asleep, in a safer place of dream, she stands over him, pushes up her sleeves, and without the laying of hands on flesh, she plays him, his body, at rest on the sofa, like a silent theremin.

With movements of her hands, flicks of her wrists, she binds him, touch-free, with invisible ribbons, ties him up as a spider with a fly would do, writes over him with inexplicable air-weave code, unknown symbols.

In the morning, she is gone. She is not in his house. He rubs his eyes, pours coffee, tops up his mug with a dash of bourbon, recalls it is his birthday. He has awoken, he has made it through.

He sighs.

There is nothing coming undone within him this morning, only a pounding headache he knows will be relieved by more of the same from the night before. A soft catatonia ripples through him. *Another day,* he thinks, *another day.*

He dresses, heads out down to the beach, in search of pairs of footprints, to confirm the dream he thought he'd had, was perhaps still in. He finds two sets, leading down to and back from the shoreline. *She had been here,* he thinks, and then knowing she had been real, he feels a pang in his chest. Loneliness. She is nowhere, now, to be seen.

Of course, he drinks today, all day, this day is no day different to any other. He drinks and cries, cries out for his mother, waits for the numbness, his friend the bottom of the bottle brings, but it doesn't seem to come, so he continues to cry until sometime mid-afternoon. It is then he hears the crash of the waves calling. He needs to be on the shore.

Will she come again, he thinks, he hopes, as he feels he may have further questions. *Perhaps if I play again, create with my hands and the electromagnetic force field of my instrument, an invisible form once more of Mother's face, or a face that bears some resemblance but is not quite the same.* So he does so. He carts his theremin, small generator, amplifier to the beach, and sits in the flat dry spot, the spot where rarely people who have lived in the desolate house he now lives in have stood or sat before to stare out to sea, perhaps to scatter ashes like he had done with what was returned to him in urns of his parents from the crematorium.

His hands, encouraged by the abyss in his sad heart, weave the sea air, curl and flatten it into hair, lips, the curve and plain and dip of her décolletage. Mother. Not quite mother. The whisky making perhaps a shambles of his precision, although he cannot yet feel the effect of the drink, despite swig after swig after swig.

He plays her again and again, to the gulls who swoop at dusk hopeful for a catch, to the seals who bask on the rocks a great stretch of water away, to the water as it hugs and retracts from the shore. But is he casting a true image of her face, he wonders. *Is this a true likeness?* He questions his own palms, fingertips. Has the vision he holds of her in his mind, over time, become distorted?

He plays as the sun drops to its position, into its soft armchair of purples and crimsons on the horizon, above the water. There it sits, kissing the water, and this is when she returns.

Walking across the bay, the lady who had been there the night before, who had come to each of his gigs at the bar far along on the next bay. The beach is his and hers alone.

He stops, his hands, arms numbed by the sight of her. She is carrying something in her arms. He watches her as she stops, kneels, releases what she has carried across the beach. It is a collection of things, all sizes. She arranges them around herself, until she is garlanded by a circle of dark bumps on the sand, right on the water's edge. She sits down in the middle.

He wants to go closer, starts to pack up his equipment, his heart yearns to ask her who she is, what she is, this creature who is familiar yet not: a passing face that smiles blankly in a crowd never to be see again or the face of all things powerful, all things recognised, combined. He is not sure.

She looks up, the last of the light enough for him to see her face. She speaks to him, "Stay, play on, play someone else, your father," she says, "that has always been and will always be one of my favorites," and he feels he has no choice, so he begins. But his father's face is not clear in his mind, all that he can capture from memory is the image of Pa furled in the kitchen, a bump, broken inside. He does his best and depicts with hands and air and swooping ethereal music what little of the shape of his father he can remember. "Good enough," she says.

He plays and he watches as she too waves her arms, stiff, then soft, welcoming then repulsive, in the last of the light of the day. She bends forwards, a sort of reiki he supposes, and one of the still things she had discarded around her shuffles, becomes a moving shadow, and scurries away into the dunes. He is taken aback, his music stops, but she commands him to play on. "Your father," she says, "or something that is not quite." His attention returns to his hands, his heart thrumming, as if it may burst. And the day is not out, there is still time for something inside him to break, he worries.

And as if she has read his thoughts, "Nothing inside you will break" she says, and he knows she speaks the truth, but he is sure the seam in the fabric of his reality is coming unstitched.

She places her hands on another mound of darkness, moves them in time, in dimension with his, the thing this time does not move, does not up and scuttle away. He watches as she tries again, whatever she is doing, he watches as he sees hers shake her head. "This one cannot be helped," she says, loud enough for him to hear, although he is sure she is talking to herself. "We give to those who can be helped and take back from those who can't."

Her posture changes, she arches her back, lifts high her hands as if stretching to pull the last of the light from the sky, and up from the heap, the body—is it an animal?—shoots forked light, like lightning, some part of the electromagnetic spectrum that he is unfamiliar with perhaps. It travels up, moves into her raised palms like distance into a retractable measuring tape, like the reeling in of a fishing line. *She is taking something from it,* he thinks. She shudders and then stands, kicks the spent vessel into the sea. Working her way around the circle, she does not touch them with her hands. Some she kicks into the sea, some scuttle or swim away.

He wants to ask her what she's doing, but she once again commands him to play, so play he does. He plays again the shape of his mother, her face in his mind clearer than Pa's, until the last wisp of purple-orange daylight diminishes, and the moon, now full, or fully open if it is in fact just a hole, is there, and she returns her energies to the final injured beast at her side, the largest of her macabre collection.

He can see now, its outline, now it is the last mound at her side.

It is a seal pup.

Over the noise he himself is generating, he hears it click and whistle and bark in distress. *Is it missing its mother*, he thinks, *or is its mother the reason it is lying here injured*, and he can't help but think this same thing about himself, as if he were there, in the place of the seal, being played upon by another, teased between a place of safety and the alternative by something that, in his mind, should be, have been, infallible.

She dances her hands around the young beast, and he watches as it lifts its head, flops itself back towards the sea, and in, in, and away.

From half-dead to half-alive or vice-versa—he cannot be sure—*this woman turns things, creatures,* he thinks. Now under the light of the moon, he is certain, this is not his mother, this collector and donator of force, not any of the good parts of his mother anyhow. Perhaps he has been playing her incorrectly.

He stops playing, places a palm against his chest, feels a throbbing there, a strong beat. "What did you do to the pup?" he asks, his voice small, fluttering.

"The pup was injured, but salvageable. I have given it the only gift I know how, for I cannot play a great music, cannot create sweet art, so I have given it a gift from my heart, the gift of eternal existence."

"What did you do to me?" he says, his voice low.

She stands, steps out onto the water, and glides forwards over the rippling surface, one soft footstep after another, until she reaches the reflection of the moon. Here, she stretches her arms above her head, gives a bend to her knee, jumps up streamlined, and dives down through the white quivering circle on the surface of the sea. And through this moment, he sees her actions reflected in the night sky, her reflection also diving upwards, towards the heavens, towards the hole in the sky which is the moon. She vanishes through both moons in unison, as if the glassy crest of the sea is in fact a mirror.

She is gone.

It is as if she was not ever really there in the first place. And it is just him now, alone.

All is not as it seems, he thinks and swigs down the last of his bottle of whisky, although he realises, despite trying his very hardest, he hasn't felt drunk all day. He packs his equipment at speed, throws everything back into the large case, and stumbles back up the path and back to his house. This beach can no longer be home.

He no longer plays, no longer drinks, as it does nothing any more to numb the loneliness which stabs at him from within. He no longer dares weave the faces of the lost to himself or to a crowd, and he no longer lives by the sea.

But he thinks he sees parts of her often, in the faces of others, the best bits of her and, more often than not, the worst, but it is never her, never quite her.

Now he is so old, so old he has outlived everyone he has ever met, anyone he has ever played for, and anyone who has ever passed him in a fleeting moment as a stranger does in the street. He is now so old the lines on his face, the seams that will hold his muddled grasp of reality together for an eternity, are deep. Deep enough to lose oneself entirely.

Extinction

Alyza Taguilaso

When viscous yolk sprung
a sky blooming so bright,
everyone knew. No ringing alarm
or cymbals clanging from spires. No drums
of war. Nothing churning
from the waters. Whales humming
to their calves in wavelengths
that meant *Sleep*. Thousands of feet below the surface,
angler fish flicking luminescent appendages
like morse code. Sand on the beach pale
as ivory. All eyes looking
upon heaven consuming
itself with its gaping mouth.
Teeth sharp and fine as memory. Gods
in the image of men. No prophet spoke
this in scripture but everyone woke up today knowing
it was time. All words exchanged. All misgivings, laid
to rest. What use were secrets in a day that wouldn't stretch
its limbs to tomorrow? Bullets lie asleep
in magazines. In our small home,
I hold your hand tightly
as the world begins
its burning. How wonderful
to have known such beauty,
such vicious laughter.
To have had just enough time

before our bones fuse
into stardust.

Auntie Shanta and the Slaughtering Process

Chris Kuriata

Deep in the acreage, I dream about the sea—mastering the hardships and discovering new worlds—until Auntie Shanta slips her hands beneath the sheets and seizes my ribs, strumming me like a harp until I awake.

"Let's take a walk, darling. Just the two of us."

The sun won't rise for hours, but Auntie Shanta muffles my protests with good-morning kisses. She wipes the crust from my eyes and pulls a dress over my head. Leaving home feels like casting off; we are drifting into the great unknown. Once the current takes hold, our vessel won't return for years, if ever.

Hand-in-hand, Auntie Shanta and I cross the field separating our house from the woods. Like the tundra or the desert, the field is so desolate you feel like you could be noticed, just for a moment, by the eye of God. I walk half-crouched, keeping watch over my shoulder, afraid the Creator will point me out to one of Their hungry, winged favorites who will swoop down and carry me off into the sky.

Auntie Shanta laughs and pokes a finger into my pudgy Buddha belly.

"Oh honey, not even a hundred birds could lift you an inch off the ground. Believe me."

She lies. I haven't forgotten walks through the woods with Grandpa. He wears a telescope around his neck, the rings permanently encrusted with salt from his time at sea. When he collapses the tube you can hear the dry brine crunch. Grandpa likes to put the telescope in my hands and aim the barrel into the trees where flashes of white peek from the lush canopies. Bones dangle from the branches—belonging to men who have fallen from a great height, likely after having the juiciest steaks stripped from their bellies. How else could they possibly have gotten up there?

According to Auntie Shanta, I'm being foolish. "Grandpa wants to make you superstitious, because superstitious girls stay home like old cats instead of heading into the world looking for adventure."

Leave it to Auntie Shanta; she knows how to challenge my ego. Desperate to prove myself more adventurous than an old cat, I charge into the woods, allowing the branches and leaves to swallow me whole, striding as fearless and confident as if our late-night walk had been my own idea.

Anything capable of thought is capable of being food. None of humanity's grand history or philosophical musings will save us from our destiny as nutrition. It isn't enough that we must die, we must also become edible. True nobility comes from recognizing your position on the food chain. Know the highest life forms are eventually consumed by the lowest.

At school, my city friends are troubled by this reality, and so they will not eat meat, believing the steak on our plates and ground beef in our hamburgers are paid for by cruelty and evil.

My experience differs. On the acreage, I put our chickens down swiftly and without malice. During a visit to Cousin Thompson's farm, I watch Grandpa help slaughter a cow. I even pitch in by leading the animal to a secluded pen, out of sight of the rest of the cattle. When the time comes to shoot,

Auntie Shanta and the Slaughtering Process

Cousin Thompson's hands won't stop shaking, so he passes the rifle to Grandpa, who fires so calmly and cleanly the cow dies as if from old age.

I have been lured into the woods by a woman who means me harm. I can't tell if Auntie Shanta has rigged a trap or if she's putting her trust in a deadly collision between the unpredictability of nature and the power of her own positive thinking, but her confident gait assures me she entered these woods certain only one of us will emerge.

Auntie Shanta exists outside of the food chain, taking meat from wherever she pleases, disrupting the natural flow between one species and another. Her contempt for nature is obscene. Unlike the rest of us, she has no intention of feeding back into the food chain. She's trying to live forever.

When I disappear, no one will take her inability to express grief as evidence of foul doing. Auntie Shanta is always stoic. Auntie Shanta is always collected. In the midst of tragedy, while others weep and rend their garments, Auntie Shanta is efficiently booking the church hall and sending measurements to the undertaker for an unusually small coffin.

Everyone admires Auntie Shanta's commitment to duty, never stopping to consider she is the cause of all our heartbreak.

Who besides the woman eschewing electricity for candlelight has the expertise lighting matches in the wind to successfully set fire to Bruce Bellows' barn? The culprit used no accelerant besides straw, yet the barn went up like a tinderbox. The fire department said the arsonist used a single match, and they could barely hide their admiration for such a talented foe.

On the acreage, workers respectfully tip their cap to a passing Auntie Shanta. Do they not remember the maggoty hunks of meat hanging in Bob Mund's supermarket? Each time the butcher split a rack, a shower of squirming white maggots rained to the floor like the bounty from Damnation's piñata. There was so much spoiled meat, Mund hauled a truckload back to his property to be buried in the most expensive mass grave in the county's history.

At school, cruel stories circulated claiming each night poor Bob Mund crawled to the dirt mound and exhumed chunks of maggoty meat for his own dinner. I thought that was bullshit until I saw him at the supermarket. Lying smack dab in the middle of the cereal aisle, standing out against the marble patterned linoleum like a shiny new quarter, was one of those maggots. Mund happened to be in the aisle with me straightening the boxes, and he spotted the maggot the same time I did. I thought he was going to step on it, but instead he pinched the wriggling worm between his fingers and popped the tiny morsel into his mouth.

Grandpa said Mund ate the maggot to show his mastery—*I'll show you ya' little business destroying son-of-a-bitch*—but I don't think so. He looked so serene eating the maggot, chewing with his front teeth in order to savor the juices. He ate that maggot like someone who had acquired a taste for them.

Mund's shoppers never considered the true culprit behind all this misfortune. Auntie Shanta's last visit to the store resulted in a horrible squabble (over an expired coupon or her grazing grapes, I can't remember which). The highway throws a lot of roadkill onto Auntie Shanta's property, so she always has maggots. Fishermen know to stop there on their way to the lake. How easy would it be for her to line her sleeves with eggs harvested from that morning's roadkill and sow them into Mund's fresh meat? Surely easier than setting Bruce Bellows' barn on fire, I can tell you that.

And finally, most damning, we have Charley Ulster's funeral.

Charley had been born early with a bad heart, but the little incubated baby prevailed. He made his parents proud, but such hope couldn't be maintained forever. Soon after his first year, he surrendered into the embrace of Eternity in his little plush cot. His mother discovered him just before dawn, and her wails woke us before the cock crow.

A coffin for a young 'un is a special order. I imagine in the old days acreage folks used to rip their medicine cabinet off the wall or repurpose a finely varnished spice rack to serve as an infant's casket. Baby Charley's stunted coffin only needed four pallbearers, and two of them were for show, supporting the weight with just their fingertips. Everyone was grief struck, the sorrow made worse by there being no obvious cause of death.

Auntie Shanta and the Slaughtering Process

Only it weren't no mystery to me. I'd been at Baby Charley's house delivering fresh berries to his exhausted mother, so I knew his nursery was located on the second floor of the house. The latch on Baby Charley's window looked busted. Anyone with stamina could climb the wall to his window, lift the sash with one hand and cover his face with a pillow. Done correctly, there would be no way to determine if he smothered himself or if someone lent an assist.

After the graveside service, the mourners convened back at the house, each bearing generous portions of food. Casseroles and meat platters. Appetites were low, so the extravagant buffet went largely untouched. With their bellies full of grief, most mourners nibbled only to be polite.

A single guest ate heartily, as ravenous as a caterpillar on a fresh green leaf, and that was Auntie Shanta. She piled her plate high with Missus Jakobsen's pierogies, ignoring the weeping around her as she savored every bite of the hand-stuffed, pan-fried delicacy.

For months, Auntie Shanta had been craving Missus Jakobsen's famous pierogies. She asked several times, but was always denied, something Auntie Shanta wasn't used to. Missus Jakobsen's refusal wasn't anything personal. Her back was too old to endure the necessary counter time. She made her pierogies for Baby Charley's funeral because cooking was the only ritual she knew how to perform in the face of such unfair sadness.

Someone as athletic as Auntie Shanta could easily reach the faulty latch on Baby Charley's window. She knew doing so would force old Missus Jakobsen back into her kitchen. An infant's funeral guaranteed pierogies. Just like that, with the application of a pillow, Auntie Shanta succeeded in turning Baby Charley into food.

While she ate, her eyes followed me around the cramped living room. She knew I had seen the faulty window latch, and her threatening gaze said, *I dare you to do something about it.* There was no place for me to hide in the sea of black suits and dresses. Auntie Shanta excelled at making others feel guilty for her sins. When she tired of tormenting me, she wrapped the leftover pierogies to bring home. She'd enjoy them just as well cold.

We've brought nothing to eat on our walk because Auntie Shanta claims such provisions are unnecessary.

"This land is generous. If we brought food, why, the woods would be offended by our lack of faith."

Auntie Shanta doesn't hold herself to the same standard. She tries to look innocent, but I catch sight of the flask in her boot. Berries hang from branches like raindrops, their colors inviting, but they are toxic or worse. As we stumble away from the path, my hollow stomach gurgles, and the real reason she denied me breakfast becomes frighteningly obvious.

On Cousin Thompson's farm, he stopped feeding his cow the night before its slaughter. No wonder the animal followed me so trusting, she expected good things to eat at her final destination.

"Isn't it cruel to starve an animal before slaughter?" I asked. Why not a last meal of chocolate-chip pancakes or whatever luxuries cattle dream of?

Cousin Thompson shook his head. "It's easier when you don't gotta worry about shit contaminating the meat if you botch cutting out the bunghole."

Dizzy from exhaustion, my vision dims and wavers, making the woods appear as if they are underwater. When I rub my eyes, Auntie Shanta fills her mouth with alcohol. She tucks her secret flask into her boot, where it clinks against something metallic. A sturdy knife. I know this blade well, have seen it in action; capable of sawing through bone.

I consider making a run for it. I'll hide beneath a blanket of pine needles and wait for Grandpa to find me through his salty telescope. Sadly, the time for escape has long since passed. I've followed Auntie Shanta as dumbly as Cousin Thompson's cow into a small clearing. A circle of trees creates a small pen.

Auntie Shanta and the Slaughtering Process

Auntie Shanta pushes my hair back. Her rough palms polish my exposed forehead, like I'm some doll she's shining up for sale.

"You like music, don't you?"

That's a silly question. Everyone likes music, from the nuns sequestered in monasteries to the cavemen banging on hollow tree logs. She might as well have asked, "You like food?"

Auntie Shanta draws her finger across my forehead. "You heard me playing my records the other night, didn't you? You wandered to the barn and peeked through the knot holes, being a little spy."

'Spy' sounds nasty. A spy reports their gathered intelligence to someone, be it a government or detective agency. I did see her in the barn, yes, writhing to music beneath the full moon, but I never intended to tell anyone—less to protect her than to protect the handsome gentleman she held in her bare arms.

"That was private. That was a moment so beautiful in its own right it doesn't need witnesses."

'Witness' is another ugly word, suggesting I'll one day address a court convened to hold Auntie Shanta to account for her many transgressions. I have no desire to tell a jury of Auntie Shanta's peers how I saw her dancing in the barn, her arms wrapped around Grandpa, her forked tongue tickling his bare chest while the coils of her hair swayed like Medusa.

I know exactly how Auntie Shanta will break down my carcass. Every part of me will find use. Hair cut off to weave into a belt, bones tossed to a beloved hunting dog. The flesh of my pudgy belly will be taken off in one strip and carried home for curing. No one on the acreage will ever suspect what became of me, even as Auntie Shanta invites them to share her table.

"I think the young lady now wishes she had been an old cat and stayed home, eh?"

There are no more secrets between us. Auntie Shanta and I have traveled too far, to a place where laws—both legal and moral—no longer apply. After you've drifted into unchartered waters, no one judges the decisions you make in order to survive.

You never shoot a cow between the eyes. The bullet misses the brain, and the animal doesn't die. A suffering animal poisons their flesh. Bad death means bad meat. When Grandpa held the rifle on Cousin Thompson's farm, he drew an X across the animal's forehead, from the horn bed to the eyes. Where the strokes of the X meet is where you fire to guarantee instantaneous death. Knowing this, Auntie Shanta drags one thumbnail across my forehead, leaving a red indentation. I can feel the slaughter X burning my skin like hogweed.

I fixate on Auntie Shanta's smooth, unwrinkled brow. She keeps herself youthful with nightly masks of mud and ground herbs, but these beauty treatments also expand her pores. I see the cluster of tiny holes in her skin, and soon a clear, vibrant X emerges, like the constellation of Taurus standing out in the night sky. I follow the lines of her natural X until they meet, seeing exactly where I must strike to save myself.

Auntie Shanta moves first, reaching into her boot.

The apron of my ratty dress is empty. I have no rifle or bolt to plunge into her X. All I have are the muscles in my calves. I tense them and I spring, flying into Auntie Shanta's arms as if I've been catapulted.

I catch Auntie Shanta off guard, but she doesn't forget her survival skills. She knows when attacked by a wild animal your best chance for survival is to go for their snout. The base of her hand clobbers my nose. I hear the bone crunch and my eyes flood with water.

Unfortunately for Auntie Shanta, I'm more vicious than a wild animal. A throbbing snout doesn't stop me. Auntie Shanta grunts, regretting not going for my eyes instead.

The skin on her neck is leather-belt tough, but my jaw has the strength of a bear trap. Her skin tastes of the lips of a thousand lovers, including Grandpa's, but I ignore the bitterness and rip into her throat, busting the soft pipes underneath. Auntie Shanta beats the back of my head with a blunt object, but dispassionately, rapidly losing spirit. After the third strike, she drops her flask. With a glug-glug-glug sound, both she and the bottle pour out from their necks into the thirsty dirt.

She sinks to the ground like a doomed ship, collapsing on top of me. With limited air in my lungs, I feel trapped. Remembering Grandpa's tales of endurance on the high seas, I cast off my panic and work to free myself. My baby teeth would have broken off in the toughness of Auntie Shanta's hide, but my new teeth are sturdy, anchored deep in my skull. I refuse to lie here, waiting to be found next spring with my corpse caged within her skeleton. I tunnel through Auntie Shanta, gnawing my way out of her depths, reaching for the surface, gasping for fresh air.

Hours later, I land on the other side of the woods, where gray chimney smoke guides me to a familiar house squatting on farmland that has seen better days.

Poor Missus Jakobsen! She scrambles through her kitchen, looking to find me a plate. She feels ashamed for not having a hot meal prepared for a weary traveler, even though my visit is a surprise.

Her four grandchildren huddle beneath the kitchen table, observing me closely, looking for signs of monstrosity. When they decide I'm not dangerous, they begin picking the burrs and twigs from my body, singing as they work.

Missus Jakobsen presents me with a humble plate of preserves and cold sausage, and I thank her profusely, not wanting her to feel any more embarrassment on my behalf, but when she takes her grandchildren to bed, I can only push the food around the plate, unable to muster up an appetite.

As the first stars appear in the night sky, I sit at the table alone, waiting for Grandpa to arrive and carry me back to shore. Both my hands try to hide the firm paunch of my stuffed and swollen belly. I remember Bob Mund crawling to the mass grave of spoiled meat, and I fear what I may have acquired a taste for out in the woods with Auntie Shanta.

I used to believe a woman of skills like Auntie Shanta existed outside of the food chain. If she ever died, the maggots would abhor her nutrients. Instead of breaking down and becoming part of nature, she would spend eternity as a hard clump of rebellious skin and deviant bones. Maybe a future civilization would dig her up and put her in their museum, mistaking her imperishable meat for fossilization.

To my everlasting relief, my fears prove to be nothing more than superstition. A breeze comes through the kitchen window, carrying the sound of a thousand tiny mouths. The lowest members of the food chain have squirmed out of the ground to cover Auntie Shanta and gobble up all evidence of our voyage through the woods. After the bugs and the birds and the tree roots have had their fill, there won't be a trace of Auntie Shanta left.

The Dark Wood Teaman

Rebecca J. Allred

THE DARK WOOD Teaman is just 4.2 miles west of wherever here is. You know because a ten-foot aluminum statue, presumably the eponymous Teaman, holds a teapot in one hand, the vital information stenciled onto its squat, round body, and beneath that:

There's always time for a spot of tea!

The teapot's spout is impractically long, stretching out into a broad, curved arrow to guide the way. With his other hand, the Teaman tips his hat toward oncoming traffic. It's short and flat with a stiff brim and a ribbon round the crown, the kind a barbershop baritone might wear. His tailcoat is so long it disappears into the overgrowth. Reminiscent of the Mad Hatter but less cordial, his mouth draws wide into a grimace, and his eyes bulge as if aghast. Perhaps he is a distant, even madder cousin, driven to insanity and decay by increments under the constant assault of alternating seasons.

Had you been fully awake, the accompanying carousel might have gone unnoticed, ensconced in the late summer overgrowth as it was, but lack of sleep and superimposed bad dreams make for distracted driving. Instead of focusing on the road ahead, you stare into the middle distance, trying not to think about where you're going or what you mean to do when you arrive, and as you drive past the statue, not looking but nonetheless seeing, you catch a glimpse of someone peeking from between thatches of tinder-ready grass and the skeletal tumbleweed remains of wild indigo tangled around its base. Someone small and scared.

More alert than you've been in days, heart racing to the tune of *what the fuck was that*, you press the brake pedal hard enough your seatbelt locks and a short trail of rubber traces the car's path as it skids to a halt.

"What the fuck was that?" Out loud this time. You check the rearview mirror then turn to look over your shoulder. Nothing moves. Nobody steps out from the brush or into the road. Not even so much as the wind stirs. And how long since you've seen another car? An hour ago? Two? Heartbeat slowing, you correct yourself. Not what, who. You saw a face. *Who* the fuck was that?

Driving carefully in reverse, you pilot the car back up the road to the turn off, ignoring probability and reason. You're tired and stressed. You were half asleep. There's no one there, and you only hallucinated a face. Almost certainly true, but the part of you that still fears God insists you investigate.

"Hello?"

No answer, but there is definitely something there. Narrow bars of light cut through grass so dry and brittle you briefly consider turning back to move the car back onto the road lest the heat from the undercarriage ignite a fire. Fascination overrules fear.

The coin-operated carousel is only waist-high and almost completely overgrown. The carousel children, their paint peeling like an eczematous rash, aren't riding zebras or giraffes, elephants or swans, tigers or dragons or dolphins. Instead, each wide-eyed, hysterical child rides up and down—or had, once upon a time—inside a plain, white teapot. Parting the grass to see better, you note one so corroded it appears to bleed.

Two of the children cling to drop rods that, despite lack of upkeep, still run perpendicular to the ground. Another grips the edge of a teapot's open mouth, peering over the lip, but remaining low to avoid the lid that hovers just a few inches above. Another child grasps a lid with both hands, legs pulled to his chest like a dying spider. He's screaming. Like the Teaman, the carousel children sport features more closely resembling fear than frolic. This is what you recognized when you weren't paying attention. The face of someone going to extreme lengths to avoid something unavoidable.

The remaining teapots are closed. There's no way to know for certain if there are more carousel children trapped inside, but you suspect there are. Each merry smile long since mutated into a silent scream. How long since the carousel had weathered beyond repair? How long since anyone had fed a nickel into its dark, narrow coin slot?

Bending to inspect the mechanism, you spot something scratched into the metal.

Be he god, or be he demon?
Save your breath for the Dark Wood Teaman
His kettles scream, and so will you
To sip and sup his loathsome brew.

Not the best endorsement. Not that it mattered. Anybody who wasn't already disturbed by the towering effigy or the morbid carousel was unlikely to be put off by a few lines of creepy pasta.

You fish a handful of coins from your pocket. Loose change you've collected from parking lots and restaurant seat cushions to feed expired parking meters or toss into wishing wells. The coins clink softly as they shuffle against one another. You pluck out a five-cent piece and thumb it into the slot. Nothing happens. You insert another. Still nothing. Unsurprised, you look to The Carousel Kid, the one who'd beckoned you with his secret angst, in the eye.

"Sorry, kiddo."

So there it is. Mystery solved. Not a hallucination but not exactly a who either. Regardless, you've probably lingered long enough. There are, after all, places to go and people to see.

There's always time for a spot of tea!

The Dark Wood Teaman is surely as neglected and derelict as the statue and carousel. Abandoned—if it's still there at all. You decide to check it out, anyway. Not because you like tea. You don't; you don't like to drink anything warmer than tap water, and even that tastes better with ice. Not because you're borderline exhausted and, if nothing else, it'll give you a chance to walk around a bit. Stretch your legs. Wake up. It's not even because you're more than a little curious to see what sort of place had inspired the creepy statue and the even creepier ride. And the nursery rhyme graffiti, of course.

It's familiar in an urban-legend sort of way, though you're sure you've never heard of The Dark Wood Teaman before. Has Dad ever mentioned it? You can't remember. Once, maybe? Years ago when phone calls were still possible and text messages consisted of more than Happy Birthday, Sweetheart, or Merry Christmas. Love You.

It takes a lot of faith to believe someone loves you when the fact of the matter is they don't even like you. Not even a little. Even when the feelings are mutual. You used to believe this must be how God felt. Humanity failed spectacularly to live up to His expectations, and still He decided to sacrifice His own perfect son so He could keep on loving the rest of His creations, imperfect and unworthy as they are. You used to believe it was the greatest sacrifice of all time. Of course, that's what they wanted you to believe. Now you think things might have worked out better for everyone if God and humanity had parted ways permanently.

In a sense, this is how you view your father now. The ultimate creator and authority, sacrificing his perfect child—or in this case, his idea of the perfect child—so he can keep on loving the disappointing, ignoble version you turned out to be.

This is why, instead of returning to the highway, you turn west. Not to quench a thirst, or take a break, or satisfy a curiosity. You're stalling.

Being someone's kid, it's not like being married. It's not like you had any choice about whether or not to accept or decline the relationship; that decision had been necessarily one-sided, and unfortunately, that's how all subsequent decisions remained. One-sided. No longer a function of necessity but of possessivity.

In recent months, you made the one-sided decision to end the relationship. You're not sure there is a word for what you want, but divorce is a concept your father is familiar with, something he'll take seriously.

"He may as well have stopped existing," Mom would say, years later. After the paperwork was signed, she'd neither seen nor heard from your father again. The only reason she knew anything about him post-divorce was from the rare instances you had grievance enough to bring him up. On such occasions, regardless of the circumstances or the depth of the resulting wound, you could count on her invariable reply. "Save your breath. You know better than to argue with your father."

Do you?

At night, and in the shower, and on long, unplanned road trips, arguments that never had or never would occur play out simultaneously on stages ranging in time from a memory of near-infancy so faint it might have been a dream—*sunlight; Mama's hand; a little plastic typewriter; Daddy's face red and wrinkled like a crumpled-up ball of paper*—to a dozen hypothetical futures, each confrontation more bitter than the last—*fog; an old man with silver hair and teeth gray and crooked as tombstones; a shotgun; a growling dog...*

Yet despite acting as the writer, director, and star of these productions, no number of replays or rehearsals ever results in winning an argument. Not with him. Not even in your own mind, where *you* are the authority and the truth is what *you* believe it to be. He lives there rent free, consuming valuable emotional resources like an in situ cancer that would, if not excised, eventually invade and metastasize.

Still. How do you tell your dad you don't ever want to see him again? How do you ask him for the daddy-daughter equivalent of a divorce? These questions vanish as you round a wide curve, and The Dark Wood Teaman comes into view.

Far from decrepit, the building is constructed from logs so huge and dark they appear almost sodden. Three circular windows, intact and free of dirt, wink in turn in the late afternoon sun, and the parking lot is newly paved, if empty. Only the roof, carpeted with the same moss and decomposing leaves that choke the gutters, looks even the least bit neglected. The chimney, however, must be clear; a wisp of blue gray smoke curls luxuriously from its stone throat. Empty lot or no, someone is home.

You park. Check the time. There's enough daylight left to spend maybe half an hour here and still make it to Dad's before sundown. Not that he's expecting you. If you arrive later than anticipated, there will be no grief in that regard.

Despite the smoke rising from the chimney, you fully expect the door to be locked, but it isn't. A trio of bells announces your arrival. Inside, there are two dozen tables, possibly constructed from the same lumber as the rest of the building, staggered across an open room. The air is neither damp nor musty, but the floorboards possess the same waterlogged appearance as the exterior.

On the wall opposite you is another door. It opens at the same time you close the one behind you, and out of the kitchen steps The Carousel Kid. Carrying a tray with tea settings for two and grinning in secret-terror, he gestures to the unoccupied tables, inviting, or maybe imploring, you to sit. Hesitantly, you oblige, choosing a table next to the fireplace, roughly equidistant from both doors.

He shuffles toward you, but now that you're sitting—now that you can look him right in his slightly-protruding eyes—you realize it isn't The Carousel Kid. It isn't a kid at all. The man's short stature and some odd trick of the light fooled you into subtracting half a century or more from the elderly gentleman.

He's wearing a coat that's too long, tails dragging behind him like a pair of dirty mops. More than once you think he might step on one and trip, but he doesn't. The boater perched atop his nearly hairless scalp, perhaps once a bright article of tightly-woven yellow straw, is now moth-eaten. A thin beard, wiry and gray, hangs almost to his knees. The Dark Wood Teaman, you presume, though he's nowhere as grand or deranged as his aluminum counterpart. Producing a tray stand from nowhere, he rests the serving tray upon it, and begins setting the table.

"No, thank you. I—"

A finger, narrow, tea-stained, and webbed, hovers suddenly near your lips. The resulting silence is a function of combined surprise and revulsion, not an act of compliance.

He meticulously places the napkin and silverware, the teacup and saucer, and finally the sugar bowl before you. He sets the other side, as if he means to join you. To ensure you drink whatever loathsome concoction is brewing inside that plain white teapot. He fills his own cup first, then tips the teapot toward yours.

Clear fluid pours from the spout. It collects in your cup without splashing or steaming. You glance at the sugar bowl. The cubes are beginning to soften around the edges, losing their symmetry and fusing into increasingly complex, non-Euclidean geometries. Melting into one another because they're made of ice. Ice cubes for the water.

The Teaman places the teapot at the center of the table and, instead of sitting, he turns and disappears back through the kitchen door.

You barely notice. You're still staring at the ice cubes. Pretend sugar cubes for pretend tea. Cold water tea because, just like your father, you don't like real tea. It's a tealess tea party, and now you know who the other setting is for. He isn't here, of course, but that doesn't stop him from speaking first.

"Wasn't expecting you."

"Sorry." The apology is out before you can even consider it. It's reflex. Part of an old, familiar script. You wince.

"Something wrong with the tea?"

"What? No. Just deciding if I wanted any sugar." You grab the sugar tongs and transfer two distorted lumps of ice from the sugar bowl to your cup.

"How's work?"

"Busy."

You take a sip. Imagine your father doing the same.

He wastes no time implying that you're either not working hard enough, unnecessary to the point of superfluousness, or—most probably—both.

"Mustn't be too busy for you to be able to take off in the middle of the week like this."

"I'm allowed to take vacation days, Dad."

"Nobody's saying you aren't. I'm just saying it's hard to understand why you'd be wasting your time driving out to the middle of nowhere if there's that much work to do."

"There's always work to do. And I'm glad you think me driving out here to see you is a waste of time."

"Now, that's not what I said."

It's not even what he meant. In reality, nothing would make him happier than for you to spend every spare moment focused on him. But that's not the point, because it isn't really him speaking right now. It's you, manipulating yourself in preparation for the final showdown when it won't matter what he says or what he means, because the outcome has already been decided. You sip the tea, hands shaking. It's not even real, and your goddamn hands are shaking.

"I came to say goodbye."

He doesn't bother to ask. You've come to confess, so he waits, allowing the silence to branch out and divide. Cultivating it with an air of feigned innocence and utmost attention, confident in the knowledge it will squeeze your heart and suck the oxygen from your lungs until you're forced to break it.

You gasp. A chunk of ice slips past your tongue, into the back of your throat and tumbles down your windpipe. Already light-headed from however long you've been unconsciously holding your breath, now you're choking. You expect the Teaman to reemerge, but he doesn't. Maybe he can't hear you. Maybe he doesn't care.

In the absurdity of the moment that death ceases to be an abstract concept and crystallized into an inevitable certainty, you've time to reconsider. Maybe the Teaman can hear you, and maybe he does care, because maybe this was his plan all along. Maybe the ice cubes were poisoned, and you're supposed to die choking on ice water tea, just like the girls in the riddle.

Daddy told you that one. He used to stump you with riddles all the time. At least he thought so. You are actually quite good at riddles; once you figured out how they differed from jokes, you were often able to derive the answers for yourself, but you only ever made the mistake of showing it—of winning—once.

"What starts with a T ends with a T and has T in it?" Daddy stooped, looming smugly over your tealess tea party, never expecting you to recognize the answer sitting right in front of you.

"A teapot!" You sprang to your feet, victorious.

Daddy stood up straight and frowned.

"Cheater," he said. "You've heard this one before."

"No, Daddy. I promise, I—"

Daddy turned and stormed out of the room, and the ice in the sugar bowl shifted in the aftershock of his retreating footfalls. In the riddle about the two girls and the deadly iced tea, one of the girls didn't die, even though she drank twice as much tea as her friend, because she drank her tea too fast. Before the poisoned ice cubes had a chance to melt.

The one in your throat does melt, shifting a bit, and it rockets out your mouth with an explosive cough, arcing through the air and bouncing to rest just outside the kitchen door.

There's barely time to catch your breath before you notice the blood. It's all over your hands and shirt, dripping down your fingers and staining the floor. A shard of fine bone china curves like a serpent's tooth from the meatiest part of your hand.

You grip it between thumb and forefinger, careful not to slice your fingertips as well. The shard slips almost painlessly from your palm. You drop it onto the table and bandage the wound with a napkin. The table is littered with the remains of a shattered teacup, melting ice cubes, and huge drops of blood congealing round the edges like the vestiges of an altogether different kind of brew.

This was a stupid idea. Not just stopping at the teahouse; all of it. You should leave. Cut your losses and go home and forget about everything. Save it for another day. Instead, you cross to the kitchen door and pause, hand pressed to the handle, ignoring the growing urge to flee. You dismiss the idea of poisoned ice cubes as the half-memory, half-fantasy of a dying brain. It's not the Teaman's fault you choked and broke the cup, and if nothing else, you should warn him about the mess or offer to help clean it up.

"Hello?"

Not a sound from the other side. No more from this side either, except for the last bit of ice crunching beneath your left foot as you push the door open.

Shadows, long and lean and carried by thin light spilling in from the tearoom, clamber down a narrow staircase, chasing away ribbons of light that emanate from some room beyond. You descend, counting the stairs on your fingers and the rapid thump of your heart in your head. Thirty-seven and one-hundred and forty-two, respectively, by the time you reach the corridor at the bottom. You allow yourself to breathe again and make the mistake of inhaling through your nose. The air reeks of shallow puddles overgrown with algae and choked with dying fish.

To hell with this.

Turning, you take the stairs two at a time, intending to drop some cash on the table and get the fuck out. You're halfway up when the door at the top slams shut, plunging you into near-total darkness.

"No!"

The word is dead on arrival, as if you'd shouted into a vacuum. Hands stretched out in front, you stumble to the top and slam your fists against the door.

"What are you doing? Let me out!"

Once again, the words fall almost soundlessly, like the flutter of insect wings lost beneath the erratic hammering of your fists. Blood trickles from beneath the napkin, tracing warm, narrow paths toward your elbow. Eyes adjusting to the dim light, you note a new smear punctuating every strike. A moment later and you can make out words carved into the wood.

> Be he man, or beast, or spirit,
> Save your breath, for should he hear it
> The Teaman's thirst will leave no choice
> His choir craves the unknown voice

Arms suddenly limp and legs threatening to follow suit, you sink to the ground. A frantic search through your pockets turns up empty, and you try to recall the last time you had your phone. At the table? Outside? In the car? Doesn't matter. All that matters is where the phone isn't.

Seeing no other choice, you press a hand to your mouth and nose and retreat back down the stairs. The corridor at the bottom is narrow, lit by flickering light from the cavern ahead. Crouching, you advance to the end and peer out into a medieval catacomb.

Stone pillars heave upward, arranged in a semicircle to support a ceiling too lofty to see, and pocked walls curve convexly outward, imparting a roundness, a sense of theater, to the space. Oil lamps occupy some of the recesses, but most hold teapots. All are positioned so that their spouts point like beacons toward the center of the room.

Moving inside, still crouched and hugging to the wall, you work your way around the chamber until you're close enough to make a break for one of the pillars. You scurry across crablike, standing at last to press your back to the cool stone. From this vantage you can now see the source of the stench which, at this distance, has become a miasma. Despite a complete lack of natural light inside the cave, the pond is reedy, its surface a mosaic of lily pads and ropes of thick, yellow foam.

On a lily pad near the far shore squats an enormous frog, easily as tall as a first grader. Blood flows from your palm as you make a fist, focusing on the pain to avert a scream. If such a thing were possible, you'd fold yourself into the rocky column at your back. You press yourself firmly against it, breathing shallow as a fish on land, and willing yourself into shadow.

You remain motionless long enough for your legs to suffer past the point of pins and needles to a numbness as cold and heavy as the stone itself. The giant frog hasn't moved either. Slowly, gently, you lower yourself until you're sitting, legs bent so you can begin resuscitation efforts.

On the shore nearest you, perhaps only ten yards away, something moves. It's almost imperceptible at first, but then a screen lights up and the cell phone's vibrations become the obvious intruder in an otherwise organic environment.

The urge to stand and sprint over is almost overwhelming; only by once again squeezing your hand until it bleeds are you able to resist. The frog hasn't moved, not yet, but it might; the phone is still vibrating, and your legs probably don't work right now, anyway.

As if to confirm this last thought, the first electric twinges of waking nerves begin a bilateral thrum. You work the muscles harder, tenderly pummeling them with your fists, simultaneously alternating the position of your toes—flex and point and flex and point—coaxing each nerve and fiber back to agonizing life. Once the thrumming subsides and you're confident again in their ability to support you, you gain your feet and resume your crablike scuttle, moving from the pillar to the edge of the pond and your best chance of escape.

You snatch it up, meaning to bypass the lock screen by engaging the emergency call option, only to drop it again, shocked to discover it's your phone. On the ground next to it are your keys, a tobacco pipe with a cartoonishly long stem, an ancient leather pouch stuffed with dry leaves, and yet another teapot. You reach again for the phone. In the otherwise unnatural silence, a faint plea rises to your ears like an echo.

"What are you doing? Let me out."

Instinctively you press the phone to your ear, but the voice isn't coming from the phone.

"Let me out."

It's coming from the teapot.

All rational thought ceases. You bend toward the teapot, breath held, and lift the lid. Clinging to it, encased inside a shimmering soap bubble, The Carousel Kid lifts his gaze to meet yours. Instead of the panicked and terrorized expression you've come to expect, his face crumples into the relieved and hysterical features of the lost child who has finally been found. The Carousel Kid presses a hand to the inner surface of the bubble, then makes a fist and strikes it just as you'd struck at the door and with much the same result.

You extend a finger, point it directly at the tormented child, and poke it forward and back, fast like a snakebite, popping the bubble. The Carousel Kid vanishes along with the shimmering membrane.

It's as if another larger bubble has also popped. The fetid air has cleared considerably, and whatever acoustic dampener had existed is gone now.

You rotate slowly in place and attempt to quantify the porcelain ensemble one chorister at a time: blue willow; pink roses; yellow roses; monarchs; blue birds; herons; bamboo. Solid colors ranging from bone white to obsidian; violet and crimson and emerald and gold; chartreuse and ochre and coral and puce. Rows upon rows upon rows without end. The teapots are screaming. All of them. Each individual spout a tiny orifice crying out for release.

Something leaps onto your back and fastens rubbery fingers round your throat. Heaving its weight, it pulls you backward into the pond. Hindered further by the added weight of soaked clothes, you flail to the surface just long enough to snatch a generous lungful of air before being dragged down again.

The pond is deeper than you could have imagined. One second you're sinking like your ankle's been strapped to a cannonball, watching helplessly as your next breath draws nearly out of reach, and the next you're floating unencumbered.

Lake grass and pondweed wave in slow motion, revealing, between alternating curtains of green, mounds of bodies and disarticulated bone. Your father stands tall among the tangle of drowned souls, hair waving gently in the current. Impatient. He's got something tucked under one arm like a football.

"Well?"

This isn't real. Lack of oxygen again, only this time it's a hallucination instead of a memory. You kick toward the surface, moving as deliberately as possible.

"Aren't you going to say it?"

No. You're going to ignore him. Save your breath and live to fight another day. You didn't almost choke to death only to drown less than an hour later.

"Or shall we say I won?"

You stop kicking and pivot in the water. You're living on your last breath and far from guaranteed the next, but you feel somehow this is the final riddle. Your last chance to give the right answer and get away.

"I've nothing more to say to you."

"Come on, now. Let me hear it."

"No."

"Why not? Isn't that what you came for."

"I said, no."

You're running out of breath.

"It doesn't count unless you say it out loud. Otherwise it won't be real, and you'll never really be free." The voice is right in your ear, repeating your own thoughts back to you.

You resume kicking, but a pair of gorgon eyes appear before you, glowing like twin stop lights and halting your progress. A few bubbles escape your lips. They jitter upward like butterflies to the sky.

"What do you want from me?"

"What starts with a T ends with a T and has U in it?"

No longer disguised as your father, the Teaman takes the item from beneath its arm and presents the teapot as it had been present so many years before. It's not the right answer this time, the riddle has changed. At the same time, you know it is the right answer. Either way, if you tell him what he wants to hear, you lose. He isn't your dad, but whatever the Teaman is, he wants the same things. Humor me. Make me feel important. Live perfectly and without complaint within the constraints of the world I've made for you.

The Teaman removes the lid from the teapot.

Solve the riddle but lose the game.

Not this time. Not now, and not ever again.

"No!" You scream, making sure that even underwater he and God and the rest of creation are forced to hear and acknowledge the rejection. Instead of surging upward, the expelled bubbles are drawn into the open teapot, and you kick desperately toward the surface in an effort to escape the vortex.

You almost make it, breaching the surface hands and arms first, your skin caressed by empty, cavernous space up all the way up to the elbow. Next, the top of your head, followed by your face and—oh, thank god—your lips and your mouth and throat, and you can breathe again.

For a few moments, that's all you do: breathe, floating and exhausted and relishing a sense of relief. Of freedom.

You open your eyes. There's a hole in the sky. It closes rapidly as the Teaman replaces the lid, but not before you catch a glimpse of your own drowned body floating forever breathless behind him. A bit of pond water slips into your mouth. You spit it out reflexively, unwilling to acknowledge the flavor.

Labyrinthine

Michael Bailey

> We are stuck
> in this waltz
> of our mind

Josh sits at his red piano, paint on his hands. Some has congealed around and under his fingernails and he's high-strung on the chemicals that define him, as well as others introduced into his system. It's chaotic, this life, both beautiful and horrendous and fragile, he thinks, then says to the echoey room, "But it's all we have," the words dancing off the walls, and he sings, "so why not share it / it'll leave you, baby / if you don't care for it."

    Damn, that's good, the 'care' in the final line stretched out long to offer weight. Catchy, sure, yes, it could work. Yes. Albeit generic, the phrases perhaps spoken enough times in common tongue to make it unplagiarizable *(is that even a word, no)*. He's about to write it all down, even scribble the made-up word. He needs to transcribe the lyrics before he forgets because sometimes words overwrite words. He's about to ink a verse or two in his somehow-not-yet-falling-apart notebook, into which all flowy words go, when the pen hesitates, the way a paintbrush hesitates before stroking, the way the blade hesitates before cutting. *Paint, blood?* They can be fragile, thoughts. Then the pen goes back to where it was before, on top of the piano, although the words hang unwritten above the paper a moment and he thinks, like the last sung words, fading, *no, 'don't care for it.'*

Someone sang something so similar, he muses, an accidental and clever alliteration, which makes him smile. "Shit, someone sang it. Before now. Before me. *Ante nosotros, mi amiga,*" he says and taps Amelia. Yes, she has a name, the piano, the way anything loved so long and so often should have a name. They'd been together ten years, his longest relationship. He doesn't want to get anymore red on her (*she's already red and gotta good* read *on her*) but wants to play her, badly, want his fingers on the white of her bones. *Te llamaré Amelia*, he'd told her long ago, *y te jugaré hasta la muerte*. She was complicated: an acoustic, keyboard, stringed percussion instrument. Yes, he'd play her till her last string gave out.

The clingy words had fallen too easily off the tongue to be original, to be *his*, and he knows this, though he wants the words as his anyway. They had to've been from a song heard a long time ago, on the radio, maybe, back when people used to listen to radios, nothing too recent; twenty, thirty years in the past. A friend of a friend of his back in New York would say it like that: *had to've*. And if that friend or even friend of a friend knew what he'd done ...

Shouldn't've done it, Josh. *Shouldn't've* done it. Gotta come up with something new now to overwrite what happened. Have to write it out in a song, cover all this wet pain—

—paint, blood?

He admires the red on his hands, some of it like polish on his nails, which matches the high gloss of the instrument he's about to play—*strings in a coffin*—and cracks his knuckles; well, tries to but only one pops, quick as a sixteenth-note. *Tenth-notes*, he quips, *these fingers*—not the expected full measure, a segment of time defined by several beats.

Bar, it's also called in musical notation, used to trap all the notes together in a single cell, like a prison, no, a *bar*, and oh how a drink sounds like a terribly-wickedly-good idea to help finish the unfinished song and drown the rest of the haunting morning. Early morning, or very late night? The single-syllable *bar* and its many, multi-meanings burn through him: like a metal rod it burns, like a child's forgotten chocolate it melts, like a ray of sun- or moonlight it warms and cools, like a place where alcohol is served—*yes, the best of the bars*—or like a restriction, *no honey not another drink you've had too many please stop*, or like a lawyer's exam or the partition in a courtroom, or as in 'to fasten,' or like to prohibit a person from doing something rash—*like stabbing, like murder, like another round after the 'last round'*—or like a counter to lean on when exhausted—*a drinking bar, yes*—or like a small segment of sheet music. That's a whole lotta *bars* and a whole lotta *likes*. Maybe that's the first line of the new song, something with a whole lotta hidden meaning behind a single, not-so-simple word.

"But what's the tune?" he says to the keys, out of tune, hands hovered over them, shaking but only because of anticipation. "What chords, what's the chorus, and what verses will tell this particular story of what shouldn't've happened? What's the *song?*"

It all starts with a note, followed by others strung together, some clinging like lovers to create a worth-repeating melody that doesn't mind sticking to the mind.

Sticky, these digits, but he wants to fingerpaint Amelia with them anyway. She won't mind. She's mostly red already. "No, you won't mind."

He knows he's onto something when he doesn't write the notes or the words down when he should but they're suddenly there the next morning light after a long blacked-out night. And that's exactly how this song is writing itself. Had he blacked out from drink? This morning, last night? No, not this time, though the drink hides certain truths.

That could be a line, too, Josh *(talking to ourselves now are we, yes, we believe so)*, poetic and rhyming and whatnot, although probably a little too pushy on the purple prose. Gotta get out of this third-person stream of consciousness.

He tends to wake, middle of the night or middle of the morning, humming a tune, and when he returns to playing, the notes are still there, as welcome as a friend sharing round after round of Jack® & Coke®—those two words, of course (*better as one, making love to each other in a glass, glass after glass*), belong to Jack Daniel's from that good 'ol black₍ₒᵤₜ₎ label *Old Time (Concierto) No. 7*. Yes, another drink. He makes another J&C, downs it because it tastes like familiar, and returns to Amelia before she leaves him.

The blood-red piano smiles flatly at his musings, her white teeth interrupted by the black toothless-like half-step interval ♭'s and ♯'s to compliment the A, B, C, D, E, F, G tones. Seven white notes and five blacks for each octave: a spine his fingers slide across.

He plays E♭ B♭ G, E♭~B♭ G, the second time holding the E♭ throughout the B♭ and holding the G-note a half-beat longer, then a quick E♭ B♭ before stepping down a bit and repeating the pattern with D♭ B♭ F... *Fuck*, that's just the first part of "Clocks" by Coldplay, he realizes, but holding the F since it sounds nice. Maybe he can do something with it, in time, 3:3 time *(no, that's not right)*, still holding the F. Add a note here, blur the lines between other notes there, still holding the F. All music is inspired by music heard; the way all written stories are inspired by stories read. It's much like a waltz, this borrowed part of a song, a ticking clock, although it's a 4:4 time signature. 120 beats per minute. An excited heart. The F fades until gone.

Josh thinks of the heart, how it can beat consistently for so long on its own over the course of so many years and suddenly be stilled or be slowed until still: *be* stilled and *be* slowed, until a person B♭-lined, opposed to doing so on its own; an ever-slowing metronome, tick-tick-tick-tick, then still. 4:4, no more. The musician: a god of the life of sound.

"*Held* until still," he says aloud, again admiring his hands. Those four syllables resonate the way a violinist carries her whole note, four beats on her bow. He imagines a fermata at the end of the measure—*the bar*—holding the note until someone shows her to let go, a conductor with his knife-baton until killing her last note. Then he remembers the rosin on her finger and the way she touched his face as though marking him before they parted ways.

An odd thing to do.

"A new song!" he sings, bringing the end up an octave.

He wears the hat, same one as always, both literal and figurative. It's a multifunction hat: pianist, composer, poet, writer of songs and all things literary: books, screenplays, playwrights. People recognize the literal hat. It's in every public picture, with his head cocked to the side, a little stubble, an expression teasing *I know something about this world that you don't, and I'll share little pieces with you through all my creations as the black mad wheel of time turns.*

Yes, a new song, a waltz for the three voices in his head, a simple yet purposeful arrangement of B_3 A_4 D_5, B_3 A_4 D_5, *one*-two-three, *two*-two three, "One lost voice, two crossed minds" then transitioning to B E♭ D, "three parley" and then—

3:4 time signature

One-two-three, round n' round; *two*-two-three, our thoughts spin; *three*-two-three, twirled and whirled. Never you, never me, what a thrill, always we. *One* lost voice, *two* crossed minds, *three* parley. One-two-three (four). (*wait-wait four?*), no don't stop, match the beats—one-two-three—*yet what's this*—*yes what's this*—hidden beat?

Ghost-like voice, distantly: "Dance that dance, *four*-ever, hand-in-hand, feet-on-feet, lest she die, once again," fading out, until gone.

One-two-three, *two*-two-three, *three*-two-three.

Spoken words. Foreign voice. New to us.

What the fuck.

1 of 3: "Who are you?"
2 of 3: "Let us be."
3 of 3: "Go away."

No response. Back to it. Focus now.

One-two-three—*yes let's dance*—*always dance*—'*ever-dance*, *two*-two-three, endlessly *three*-two-three. Ticking clock: second hand (slices time), *snick-snick-snick;* minute hand (hammers down), *tick-tick-tock;* then the hour, *click-tick-clang! click-tick-clang! click-tick-clang! click-tick-clang!* Clock strikes four, nothing more.

Fuck was that?

1 of 3, stern this time: "Who are you?"

Ghost-like voice, faraway: "Who am I?"

2 of 3, shakily: "Yes-yes, who?"

Ghost-like voice, still quite far: "Vanished twin."

3 of 3, lost in thought: "Vanished twin?"

Ghost-like voice, drawing near: "Three, but now (four)."

Stutter-step, *one*-two-three, slight slip-step, *two*-two-three, fluttering, *three*-two-three (misstep), palpitates, come on now, count them out, we shall dance, just us three—

Two Joshes wash four hands in the sink until the last of her is gone. Can't write a damn song with her sticking around, no. Kool-Aid swirls of pink circle the drain—one-two-three-*fuck!*—translucent pink then clear. They look in the mirror, which is cliché to include in a narrative to describe character(s), he knows, yes, he knows this well, but the reflection has a smudge under his nose and so must the reflected. Could be coke dissolved under a slightly runny nose, for a cold still lingers; could be something else: *her*, third-chair violinist working her way up the ranks. While teaching Josh some basics, she'd improved, moved up a chair, then told him there wasn't enough time for lessons, though he pleaded. Oh, those eyes when he pleaded …

She slid that small finger of hers across the rosin that had fallen with her, touched the spot just under his nose: *boop*. The first and only time she'd touched him.

One Josh touches the same place with his right index finger, just as she had, and the other Josh with his left. Both bring it to their mouth to taste, although neither knows the taste of resin. The two Joshes separate, one going to the music room, the other disappearing, for now; *there,* but not. Perhaps when the door closes and the lights turn off, a third Josh keeps him company, the two of them talking, all private-like—a reflection of a reflection in the dark, sharing secrets.

A new door opens to instruments: a drum set, three functional guitars with varying numbers of strings, a broken bass, banjo, keyboards *(plural, always plural, other lovers),* xylophone, tambourine, flute, mandolin, and violin. He's played them all, same way he used to play with toys as a child, eyes filled with excitement. A yearning to learn. Some he's great at, like the guitars and keys, of course, and some just okay, and others, well, they make noises the way people do when putting hands and lips to them. There are others, but he goes to the violin.

Inside the case is a small container of rosin. It's hard as stone, so why had it left a smudge? He mimes the girl's final action *(first person instead of third)* but after his finger waits under his nose long enough to smell pine, he puts the tip to his tongue. *Well?* It tastes like tree sap, bitter yet *ancient,* how old age and convalescence might taste if placed into a tiny container to later strum notes on a string. It tastes like the remnants of what she'd smudged him with, so perhaps her rosin had reverted to resin in the hot morning sun.

She'd marked him, *boop.*

You did this, she'd said before silence.

He makes another drink a while later with a lot of J and splash of C. One turns to two turns to three and then four. It's not yet noon but there are no 'official' rules for drinking, just whatever feels right to the drinker, and *this* feels right. He drinks until the image of her finger reaching up to touch him is gone, until her glossy eyes fade, until he finds himself once again at his red piano, Amelia, this time pounding a lower-octave F key in 1:4. 60 beats per minute and willing his heartrate to match: *Fuck. Fuck. Fuck. Fuck.*

1:4 time signature

One. Lone. Drunk. Down. Sad. Gloom. Cold. *Thoughts?* Some: lost, woe, death, harm, self, through, done, kill, soon. *Notes?* Yes, few: blue, sole. Dreams: dance, *two, three, four.*

The signature's wrong, all wrong. This new song can't be in 3:4 because there are more than three in the song, this story: Josh, his reflection, his reflection's reflection, and *her.*

Four notes are required, so he plays a 4:4 fourth- to fifth-octave sequence of F_4 A_4 D_5 E_5 on the whites, which sounds creepy as shit when played to match his slowed beat-per-second heartrate. He holds the fourth note another tick, tick, tick, tick, along with his breath—heart palpitating as though sick of the note, done with it—before repeating the pattern lest it drive him mad. F A D E. Yes, that's okay. Perfectly okay to fade. A start, anyway. How *all* songs begin, or *should:* by experimenting with order, with pace, or entirely by accident *(a misplaced hand, an ill-timed push, yes that sometimes happens).* Sometimes what happens is only an accident, right? Or are accidents purposeful? The last note, it sounds so *wrong, wrong, wrong!*

He presses the F instead of swearing, three times, and holds it.

A last note can linger, can burrow into the mind, can haunt. Shouldn't've done it, Josh. *Shouldn't've* done it. He plays the first four notes again mostly to get rid of the lingering note and because repetition can often help determine what comes next. 60 beats per minute, nice and slow. F A D E, and when he plays the last note, it stays around far too long.

"The four of us are dying," Josh says aloud, and so he switches back to 3:3 and the prior B A D, B A D, and sings, "Just us three / don't you see," transitioning to the original E♭ B♭ G, "labyrinthine?" And that could be the name of the song: "Labyrinthine," like the maze of his mind, with or without the punctuation. Could be a question or a statement. "Three syllables, as it should be" *(shit those are both four).* The G stretches out as he contemplates the possibilities. "All it needs," he sings in E♭ B♭ G. "Gee," he says, in the same tune as the note.

He imagines dancers matching the beat, *feeling* the song more than hearing it, circling round and round a ballroom in a swirling waltz. *One*-two-three, *two*-two-three, *three*-two three. Twirling round. Yes, that's it. Smooth, smooth, smooth. But the violinist and her delicate reaching hand adds a fourth unwanted note, and it shouldn't be there.

"Don't you *see* me?" he sings and plays, the words there on their own, *her* words, not his. *C?* Josh's finger slips on the next measure and plays F A C E, her face suddenly there, burned into him, which he shakes off and corrects to F A *D* E on the next go'round, suddenly back to 4:4 with her last haunting note, and he shakes his head for not getting it right. A 'fad' without the last, he thinks, without *her*, without her gaze, and stabs D$_4$ hard near the middle of the piano to kill the persistent E and those ever-staring *eyes*. "Yes, I *see* you." Three notes plus one.

"Won't you bleed out," he says, his words this time, not a question but a statement, "Won't you stay still. Won't you just *fade*."

No, not until the fourth is gone can there be a waltz, he tells himself. She's still here … washed off his hands but still here, like the itch under his nose.

Another drink or two or three or four.

4:4 time signature

Now this feels odd, the four of us, dancing like this. More like a march, or a box-step, than fluidity, than elegance; crossing the veil, toward our death. There's no finesse, no round and round, so what's the point? Who takes the lead? And who is led? Not much to it. Just one more beat. Does the fourth add? Does it subtract? A hiccup-waltz, one-two-three (four).

1 of the 4: "Why are you here?"
2 of the 4: "Why do you stay?"
3 of the 4: "Why won't you go?"

4 of the 4: "A final dance, you owe me that, 'least you can do. Just *one* more note, *two* remember; you *three* took mine, and left me *four*—"

1 of the 4: "In each measure."

2 of the 4: "4:4 four beats."

3 of the 4: "We all get that."

4 of the 4: "Won't forgive you—"

Not that we care. A final dance, and then you leave. *One*-two-three (four). *Two*-two-three (four). *Three*-two-three (four). *Four*-two-three (four).

(it's not so bad, what-what we did, no not so bad)

4 of the 4: "Sing my sad song, don't forget me. Play my sad song, play it in key. The crime you've made, write that sad song, and don't let me—"

FADE.

Not enough words, not enough time, not enough keys, not enough rhyme. What are the lines? What is the pace? What are the notes? What is this place? In harmony, remember the—

FACE.

One-two- three (four).

(we are dancing, the four of us, soon to be—)

Josh sits at his red piano, blood no longer on his hands. Was it blood? He can't remember the details, only that a new song wants out of him. A waltz. Three notes per measure. Three syllables per line. *One*-two-three, *two*-two-three, *three*-two-three. Yes, a waltz. He writes it all down: the notes, the ♭'s and ♯'s, even scribbles the title, and finally the lyrics into his somehow-not-yet-falling-apart notebook, when the pen hesitates, the way the hand hesitates before grabbing a blade. He wonders if four beats might be needed. So much can be buried in a fourth note. His thoughts bleed. They can be fragile, thoughts. Then the pen goes back to where it was before, on top of the red piano, Amelia.

All he can think about is a single lost note—

1:4 time signature
End.

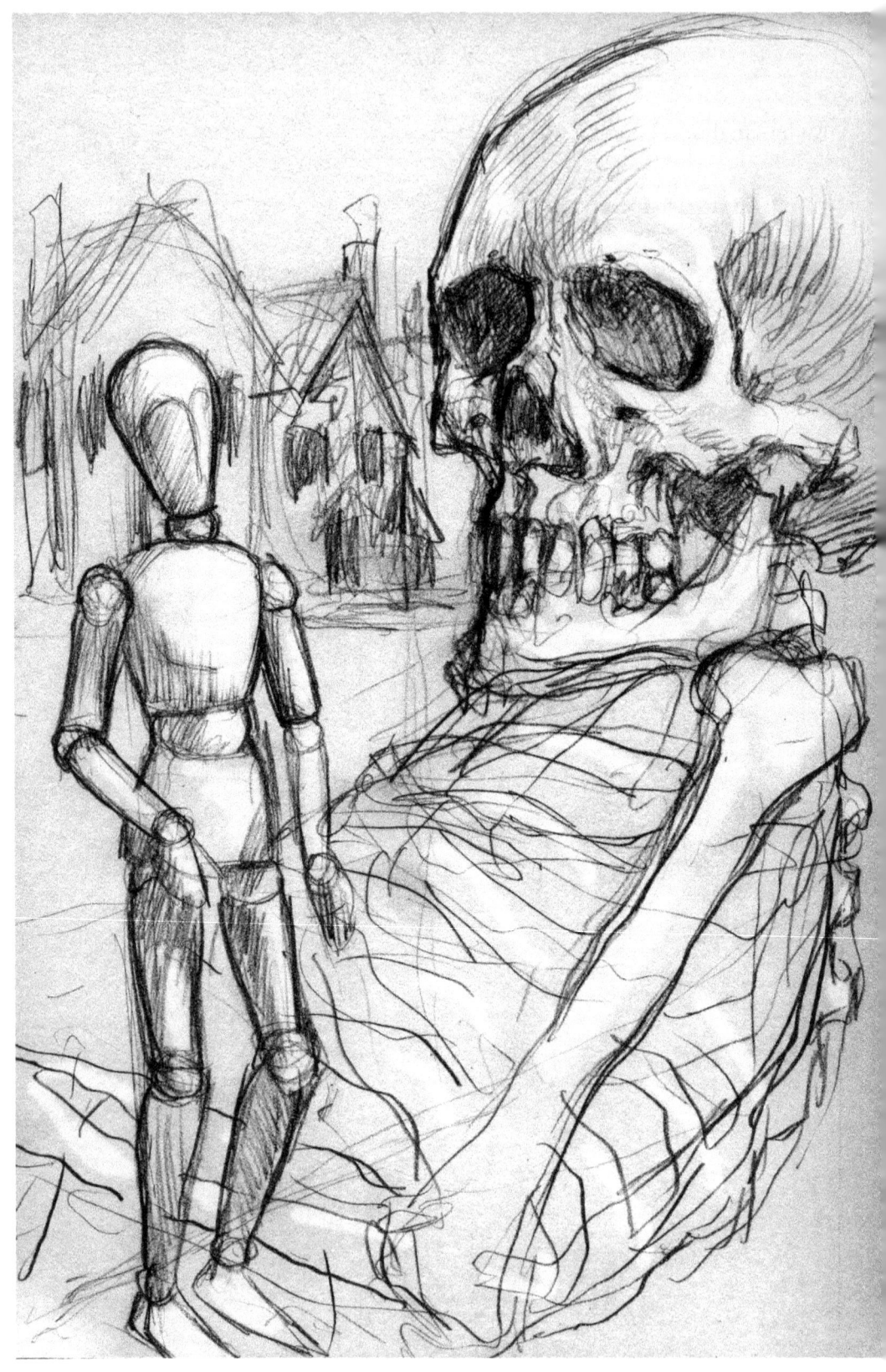

Everything Wrong with Me

Carson Winter

When I moved to the new town, I was escaping. That's all it was, really—I needed to escape. The people at home weren't nice to me. They were hurting me, they were saying cruel things. I would cry and they would laugh and jeer and they would savor the taste of my humiliation. So, this is what I did.

On my eighteenth birthday, after the party was thrown and my family and friends had finished with their subtle jabs, I went to bed smiling, knowing that this would be the last time they would ever see me. I'm sure they didn't think about it, that I would've gotten so fed up. They didn't think about it at all and as they were sleeping off their stupor, I packed. I left in the middle of the night to find a train station and I left with the intention of not knowing where I'd end up, because it didn't matter. Only that I was away.

I closed my eyes on the nearly empty train and went to sleep and when I opened them, it was morning and I didn't know where I was, only that I was away.

Where did they think I went, I wonder?

Did they care?

I pulled my luggage from above the seat and smiled at the attendant and told him to have a good day.

"You too, miss," he said.

The new town was sunny and full of fallen leaves, orange and red and brown. The new town was filled with old brick buildings and a big clock tower. The people in the new town were welcoming, they waved at me and said hello when I walked by, which I liked a lot. It made me feel as if I belonged already.

In no time at all, I had a job. It was easier than everyone made it sound.

There were signs everywhere looking for help. So, I marched myself into a small bakery and asked to see the manager.

I always liked sweets, but not because of the taste, I thought they were beautiful. They had a gorgeous sheen to them, glossy and seductive. They were also forbidden. Everyone used to yell at me when I reached for one. *No, no, you can't have that. You mustn't, you'll become too fat and that would be awful.* Well, I never cared if I got fat. I never cared about the taste at all. I just liked the idea of swallowing something beautiful.

When I walked in, a young woman greeted me with a smile. "Hello, welcome," she said. "Is there something I can help you with?"

"Yes," I said. "I'm looking for a job."

"Have you any experience?"

"No."

"That's alright. What's your availability?"

"Anytime."

The girl nodded and left for a moment. A man walked in. He was a little taller than me and perhaps twenty years my senior. He was handsome, if not slightly confused looking. "Who is this?" he asked.

"Laura," I said.

"She's looking for a job," said the girl.

"Can she work?"

"We don't know."

The man shrugged. "I'm sure she can learn."

I nodded. "Yes, I can learn. Absolutely. That's what I'll do. I'll learn."

He looked at the girl beside him, who beamed up at him with emerald eyes. "Okay," he said. "You can work in the mornings. Come by tomorrow, early, and we'll put you to work."

Really, it was that easy.

Everything went so well. That was the good part. The girl at the bakery was named Polly and we became friends very fast. Then, she introduced me to her friends and suddenly I was surrounded by people in the new town. The bakery was a good place; I liked it. And after work, we'd all go to a local hang-out, a church of sorts.

I was staying with Polly, and I knew it was her church so I was always very respectful. I never considered myself religious, but I didn't mind it so much. Sometimes it was all very pretty, and I wished I could have a rosary or pray to the Virgin, because again, I really like beautiful things—but this was not that sort of church.

After work, in the early afternoon, Polly and I went to the strip mall it was located in and waited for her friends.

"This is where we hang, you don't have to believe anything to go here."

"No? They won't mind?"

"Not at all. It's just a place and places can be anything if you think about it."

"As long as no one will mind. I don't want to be a bother."

And then something strange happened. Polly laughed, like she couldn't control it at all.

"Did I say something funny?"

Polly held her hand over mouth. "No," she said. "No, no. Well..."

"Yes?"

"Well, you're always worried."

I paused, suddenly uncomfortable. "Is that bad?"

And then Polly looked at me with her beautiful emerald eyes and said, "No, not at all, Laura. That's not bad at all. It's just what makes you *you*."

I hugged my arms around myself. She was just saying things, the way all people say things to fill the air when there's nothing else.

When her friends came—my friends, I had to remind myself—everything was fine, and I was just having fun again.

The church was full of fun things to do. We painted, crafted, watched movies, and talked. I didn't have to take part in any religion, but they did pray for a moment and I decided I would pray too, just to see what it was like.

I thanked the Creator for my new town, which I liked very, very much.

The church was a peculiar one because while it had staff, I didn't know who the religious leader was. I didn't know much about church, but I knew that somebody had to be a pastor or reverend. Someone in the building had to be in charge.

When I asked Polly who the boss was, she laughed at me again. "Boss?" she said. "There's no boss here."

"Well, you know, I mean a pastor or someone."

One of our friends shook her head. "There's no pastor here."

"What do you mean there's no pastor here? Who's in charge?"

"We are," said another friend, who could barely suppress a cruel giggle.

"What does that mean?"

"We're a collective."

"I thought it was a church."

"It's both," said Polly who now was laughing between breaths. "How did you not know?"

"I just thought that there'd have to be a pastor too. It can be a collective and still have a pastor, can't it?"

One of the girls said: "Laura, you seem really worried about this." This caused another uproar of laughter.

"I'm sorry," I said. "I don't know what I did."

"You didn't do anything," said a voice. "It's just who you are."

"You worry a lot."

"That's who you are. You're a worrier."

I felt tears, hot and salty, welling in my eyes, making them glassy and distorted in the strip mall church.

"Oh, don't cry," said Polly, voice tinged with disgust. "Don't cry. We were only joking." She sneered at me. "There's no reason to act like that. This is a church, after all."

"Yeah, this is a church."

"A collective," one said with a laugh.

"Both!" another said.

"You're being cruel," I said, sputtering. "You're not being nice to me at all. You're all being rude. I didn't know anything about this church. I've never been to church before. My family never took me to church when I was a girl. This place is new and I don't know anything about this place."

They looked at each other with straight faces and sighed.

"We're sorry," said Polly finally.

"We're all sorry."

"We were being rude."

"We know not what we say."

"Perhaps we can pray together?"

I wiped my nose and nodded sharply. "Yes, I'd like that," I said. "I'd like that a lot."

The women formed a circle, our arms interlocked, and we all bent our heads and looked to the floor. Polly was the one that spoke. "We pray to you, Creator, to bring peace to Laura. She is a good spirit with so much love to give.

She is often worried. She can't help it. But, if in your kindness you could cure her of this, we would be most thankful. Amen."

"Amen," I said, choking.

At night, Polly's apartment was quiet.

We walked home from the church, and it was like nothing had happened. She talked to me easily, in the same way she talked to me at work. It was as if she couldn't tell that I cried at all. As soon as we got home, our lives broke into routine.

She would separate from me and read. It had to do with her church. There were materials if I wanted to learn more, she told me. Truthfully, I just wanted to lay in bed.

"I'm not feeling well," I said.

"Suit yourself."

In minutes, sleep came as a welcome release. An end. I thought it was a lot like death, but better, because sleep was not forever. At its best, it was just enough.

At work, I did my best to keep up with a busy day. Sleep had cleansed me because that's what it always did. There was a moment though, when I felt unclean, but it was only a moment.

In a brief respite from customers, Polly and I worked side by side cleaning the counter. She said to me, "Why did you come here?"

I swallowed. "The people at home weren't nice to me. They didn't like me and would constantly remind me of it. It became all I was to them. So, I picked up everything and left."

Polly considered that for a moment. "What were you to them?"

"What?"

"You said it was all you were to them. What is 'it?' Was there something specific they didn't like about you?"

There was, of course. But I didn't want to say it. "No," I said. "Just small things. We just weren't a good match."

"You weren't a good match for your family?"

I turned to face her. "No, I wasn't."

"Well, you're a good match here." Her voice was warm and soft. "We love you here. You're like a sister to us."

"Really?"

"Oh yeah. We love you, Laura. Don't you know that?"

"I love you guys too," I said.

She poked me playfully in the side. "We're going to the church later, are you coming with us?"

I was flying high. "Of course," I said. "Of course."

Polly smiled serenely at me, her thin, platinum hair as wispy as a spider's web. She was an angel. When she looked at me like that, I felt like the new town was my home and I could stay there forever if I wanted. That I could be happy.

When it was finally time to leave and the owner had told us we did well, Polly grabbed me by the arm and urged me forward. "We've got to go," she said. "It's a special day at the church."

"Why is it special?"

"They're reading people. There'll be initiations, if you want."

"For me?" I did not know what it meant to read people, but I was afraid to ask lest I found out I was supposed to know all along.

"Only if you want. But it is an honor. Most people would be delighted. They'd be on their hands and knees and praising the earth I walk upon. They'd cut their wrists and give their own blood to be a part of my church." She said this savagely, her eyes shining bright.

"I *am* honored," I said, quickly. "So, very, very honored. I just hadn't considered joining. It hadn't crossed my mind."

She rolled her eyes. "We know exactly what crosses your mind," she said, softening. "And that's why we want to initiate you. To help."

I didn't know what to say so I tried to match the serenity of her smile. I smiled so hard that I felt like my lips would split a seam in my cheeks. We walked to the church, and she told me all about it, while saying absolutely nothing. She told me how the church made her feel, the ways in which it made her life better, the friends she met through it, and the people who were all happier now that they'd been. But there was no discussion of beliefs, no talk of thought-leaders or dogma. The church was like any other church, I decided, but stripped of all aesthetic. There was no mythology to this church—but it held the same function. There were no stories to tell of this church except personal stories, of friends and family who went.

In some ways, I felt like I was having a hand in building this church's mythology from the ground up. There were no stories of baby Jesus, but there were stories of how the church made me feel when I thought I was all alone. This sounded nice to me, but I didn't dare say it aloud. I didn't know if Polly thought of these things in the same way and I didn't want to offend her.

In the parking lot, Polly said, "Everyone's here already."

"Great."

She pushed open the doors and everyone's necks spun on a swivel to look at me. Polly was right, everyone was there. I felt a surge of panic and I thought of turning the other way, to run, but Polly's grip was forceful. "Don't be worried," she said.

I was pushed into the crowd, an ambiguous action. I couldn't tell if it was an act of aggression or not. Was I being thrown to the wolves?

But as soon as I was among them, it was as if I were forgotten. It was a banquet, and everyone was eating and drinking. They talked amongst themselves and some of our friends waved, familiar faces amongst a crowd of nobodies. I hadn't realized how big the church was, I didn't know many of these people. I didn't know how they could fit so many people into such a small space, but I suddenly felt like everyone I'd ever met in the new town was right there.

What is happening?

Why are they all here?

What am I supposed to do?

(I still felt as if there should be some leader here, someone who could take control. The church, to me, with its discordant orchestra of voices, felt like distilled chaos.)

This went on for so long that I was covering my ears after a while. Every time I turned toward an exit, there was a strange person standing in my way. They'd look me up and down and laugh at me. And I could barely hear their laughter because everyone else was talking.

I darted between people, running between rivers in the crowd until I found Polly.

"I need to go. This isn't fun for me," I said. "There's too many people."

And Polly's lip curled. "All you do is worry," she said. "That's all you do, isn't it?"

"I—I—"

"Always worrying. Laura, the worrier."

"I can't help it!" I screamed. "I can't help that I worry!" and as soon as I screamed it the crowd went mute.

The only thing we could all hear was my breathing.

I could feel their body heat all over me.

At that moment—I hated the new town, I hated the church.

"We know all about you," someone said finally. "We can read you."

"What do you know?" I asked.

And all together, like a chorus, they said: "You worry!" and laughed in congratulations to themselves.

"I worry sometimes but I'm not just that," I said, the words falling out of my mouth like runny vomit. "I'm a lot of things. I like things and don't like things and sometimes I'm shy and sometimes I'm not. I can look people in the eyes when I talk to them. I can sing too. See?" Desperately, I sang scales of la-las. "I'm not just someone that worries. I'm more than that, I think. Aren't I? Aren't I more than that?"

The crowd was silent for a long while and my eyes were closed tight.

Then, a woman said, jovially, "There goes Laura, always worrying."

Polly reached out to touch me and I backed away. "You can be a part of this if you want. It's a great place. We can be like sisters here, like a family."

I shook my head, cheeks flushed with rage. "I don't want a family," I said. "I left my family, and I'll do it again."

And that's when I ran.

I didn't have to leave in the middle of the night this time. I found the train in broad daylight. The sunset was beautiful, and I remembered that I liked beautiful things. I was all alone for a moment, and I remembered how great being alone felt. I liked it. It was better than the alternative.

Sometimes, I'd see someone looking at me. Someone from the new town, snickering. Reminding themselves that they knew exactly who I was, what I was all about. I didn't like that, but I knew I didn't have to see them ever again.

When the train screeched to a stop, I looked out on the new town one last time, all red brick and serenity. I didn't like it one bit. But there were other towns.

On the train, the ticket taker traveled down the aisle. "Ticket, please."

I handed her my ticket, which she took and examined carefully. "Lovely, dear. Thank you."

The new town was drifting away, gone forever, and I felt a weight lift off my shoulder. There would be other homes, I decided.

"How long until the next stop?"

"Four or five hours. But if we run late, I'll be sure to let you know."

"That's not necessary."

The old woman smiled at me, sweetly, like a kind grandmother. "I just wouldn't want you to worry, dear."

She walked to the back of the train, and I sat rigid in my seat. As trees and sunsets and beautiful things dashed by me in a blur, I prayed to a new god, and I prayed for good places.

The Great Everything of Dust

César Dávila Andrade
(translated by Jonathan Simkins)

Of the Great Everything of dust, the sun and the pineapple
and the sense that presses
against the wall of the adjoining star and
hope like an apprenticeship
of the nose in the yarn of hell,
we know nothing. We are tinted inside the dark
by hands contrary to our own
to discern ourselves in the beyond.
And brimming with infinite grains of rock, we slumber
on the stones that guard
us from the Sky.
Aldebaran, your pendants pass in soaring flights
over the granulation of species while
the sense of omnipresent weight
gyres amid the jaws and seas.
The great thoracic bullet reconciles us to our heart
every night like an eclipse,
O man, you who live as a freeloader on the façade
of your house of lime, on whose fixed eyes
the lofty necklaces of Sirius descend
to other collars and are dust.

EL GRAN TODO EN POLVO

Del Gran Todo en polvo, el sol y el ananá
y el sentido que se oprime
contra la pared del astro medianero y
la esperanza como un aprendizaje
de la nariz en hilo del infierno,
nada sabemos. Estamos pintados dentro de la oscuridad
por manos contrarias a las nuestras
para reconocernos, más allá.
Y llenos de infinitos granos de roca, dormimos
sobre las rocas que nos
vigilan desde el Cielo.
Aldebarán, tus collares pasan en altísimos vuelos
sobre la granulación de las especies y
entre las fauces y los mares
se arremolina el sentido del peso universal.
La gran bala torácica nos aproxima cada noche
a nuestro corazón como a un eclipse,
hombre que vives arrimado al frontis
de tu casa de cal, los collares altísimos
de Sirio, llueven sobre tus ojos fijos
a otros collares y son polvo.

Acts of Desperation

César Dávila Andrade
(translated by Jonathan Simkins)

When the rain fell for weeks and that vestibule
roared with blasphemies of stream and horse,
and the stars contorted themselves,
we were driven out
behind the armoires of the Flood,
and hung from the colorless cords of fetuses.
Newly drowned,
we now bore the rumbling bulk
of the children of animals and mud.
Later still the radiant outposts of the market returned.
It was possible to break out
and traverse the darkness enveloping their expeditious births.
But our execution had already been postponed.

ACTOS DE DESESPERACIÓN

Cuando llovía durante semanas y aquel zaguán
rugía blasfemias de torrente y de caballo,
torcíanse las estrellas,
éramos ahuyentados
detrás de los roperos del Diluvio,
y se nos suspendía de la incolora cuerda de los fetos.
Recién ahogados,
teníamos ya el peso retumbante
de los niños de animal y de lodo.
Volvían después radiantes estaciones de mercado.
Era posible salir
y atravesar la oscuridad que rodeaba sus veloces cumpleaños.
Pero, ya nuestra ejecución había sido postergada.

The People Upstairs

Ben Larned

It was the fucking that woke Jean – not the vibration she heard first, delivered in color rather than sound. When she opened her eyes, she recognized it for the filth that it was.

THUMP. THUMP. THUMP.

The pounding bed frame drove needles into Jean's spine. The fucking always started this way, percussing faster and faster until moans took over, then the overwrought climax. At least her upstairs neighbors were consistent. She had no idea what they looked like, but after listening to their coitus for half a year, she had some guesses. Their endurance, for one, meant they were in good shape. And beautiful, they had to be beautiful.

Her eyes strained to see the green microwave clock: just after 3 a.m., far past the hours of decency. She knew that she could ask them to keep it down. Her neighbors likely had no idea they made her so miserable. *But if they're this bad now*, she argued, *what'll they do if they know I can hear them?*

Tonight they were breaking their record. She wondered with a plasmic chill if this was their new standard, if the fucking would last longer and longer until it was all she could hear. In retaliation, she sent waves of anger toward the ceiling, hoping they would soak through the concrete, infiltrate her neighbor's lungs like a fast-acting cancer. The landlord might find them in a week, swollen and conjoined, no longer her problem.

Even better, you could stop it now – go upstairs and pound on the door until they open it and slur, "What the hell?" Present a knife in answer, ignore their pleas for mercy, luxuriate in their dying fluids. Your troll-face will be the last thing they see.

But there was a united howl of climax, a few muffled words, a final creaking of the bed. The only sound left was Jean's breath, apoplectic carbon that she hoped would suffocate her.

Signing this lease had felt like a major achievement. After four years of college roommates, Jean wanted her own place, in her home city. By the time she made it there, all she could afford were the older, decrepit buildings southeast. The size and gloom didn't bother her, if it was temporary; she would find a better place when her life truly began. If the people upstairs didn't kill her first.

The more time that passed, the more Jean accepted that such an outcome, no matter how depressing, was only natural. She had realized some time ago that she was no more than a stain on the universe, an accident or worse, better off sealed in her own corner. She didn't mind that no one in her city remembered her name. It was just as well if it meant they would leave her alone. But the old fear crept back, as she tunneled to sleep, that it was her fate to be bothered to death.

The next day's weather was suitably befouled. March in her city was wet and ugly, all scattered snow that melted fast into mud. People lost their self-sufficiency on days like this. At least it meant they had a need for Jean.

She'd been driving for a rideshare since graduation, as a bridge between jobs. The work made no use of her degree, but it gave her the illusion of authority; she liked playing the indifferent chauffeur, cataloging mankind's sickness from her front seat. Her customers, mostly transplants who worked for a start-up or dispensary or their parents' firm, needed service. They were all conceited or nasty, often both. As each of them left her car, she thought about slamming the gas, cranking the wheel, rolling her tires over their bones. *The fucking,* she'd cackle as they arrested her, *the fucking made me do it!* The previous ride had taken her northeast, an industrial district where abandoned factories had been left to rot. She decided to make this her last ride.

A notification pinged – "Request for Ride!" Jean's body throbbed with reluctance as she claimed it. She considered it a form of self-punishment, to keep going when all she wanted was to collapse; one of the few college lessons she'd put to good use.

There had been a mistake, she assumed, when she arrived at the new pickup. The passenger's address was a long-gutted compound, skeleton pylons jabbing to the sky, grounds littered with rust and debris. With a hot sigh, she checked the app for a phone number. The field was blank – the passenger hadn't filled in their profile.

Panic cemented her to the seat. How had they called for the ride in the first place, and could they be traced if something happened? She considered canceling the ride, but her ratings were low as it was. *Get fired or die,* she concluded and barked a laugh.

Someone rapped on her window so sharply she assumed the glass had cracked. The hand was pale and bony. She thought of locking her doors, but the face smiling in was pleasant, half-concealed by round mirrored glasses. He folded his body, long and sleek in a gray overcoat, into the backseat. He looked middle-aged and frail, no more of a threat than the others.

"Thank you so very much," he said as he buckled in, voice high and authoritative like an absent-minded doctor. "It is important that I make this appointment."

"Alright," Jean replied, hoping that would end the conversation. As she rolled away from the factory, the man turned to an upper window and waved.

The GPS led them toward I-70, a clot of jammed, furious drivers. Jean's chest constricted, and as she exhaled a bony finger prodded her shoulder.

"Would you mind terribly if we went a different way?" the passenger droned. "These devices get confused, you know. I'll instruct you myself. Take this left if you will. Just up here."

Her shoulder itched where the passenger had touched it. She took the left and turned up the radio.

"No music if you don't mind."

Jean held back a sigh and tapped it off. Without noise, she could hear the passenger's every movement – tapping legs, rustling clothes, nails scraping cuticles. Her shoulder blades retracted into each other.

"How long have you been charioteering this wide city?"

Jean twitched – the voice sounded close, right at her ear, though the passenger hadn't moved. "About three months," she said.

"You must know it very well. Is this your career?"

"No," she blurted. "It's just for now. With the job market the way it is…"

"A shame," the man sighed. "What is it that you *want* to do?" A customer asked her this at least once a week; as always she mumbled, "I'm not sure yet." They wouldn't understand the honest answer – *I want to be left alone.*

"Ah, yes. There's no space to know what you want anymore. You can't even feel the ground beneath your feet."

The passenger's tone classified him for Jean: a middle-aged nobody who thought he knew everything, spouting advice to anyone who couldn't walk away. Her shoulders pulled tighter, her knuckles clenched on the wheel.

"No peace, no space," the passenger clucked in disappointment. "No wonder you don't know what you want. One must seek deeper than the earth and the sky if they really want to understand. One must know where to look and what to ask. Turn left up here." As she sped northwest, he added, "Do *you* know what I mean?"

He grinned like the host of a children's show. She gave her answer low and sharp – "No, I don't."

"Of course not," he laughed. "Since you're helping me so much, I'll give you a hint. Have you ever looked into your pupils, Jean? Not the iris, mind you, there's no truth in that color. But deep in the pupil, there is another hue. Have you seen its imprint, Jean?"

How does he know my name? It was on her driver's profile, of course; unfair that she couldn't know his name in return.

"A left past these houses," he said.

The turn brought them into another development, the same as the others, only it hadn't been finished. The houses, framed to be large and fancy, had started to decay in their neglect. She wondered if this was the suburb she'd read about, where the construction crew had dug up a girl's body, freshly dead under eight feet of virgin soil. The girl's death remained a cold case, and the houses lingered half-built. Even like this, they were out of Jean's price range.

"When your nature is open, you can perceive it," the passenger clacked on. "To open one's nature – it can be a difficult, dangerous thing. It means your emotions become material, secrete out of you like fluid, take on a life of their own. Your thoughts leave odors and stains on the mind, Jean, and those stains linger in the eyes. That's why you must look into the pupils. Down that inner corridor, you will find the Empty Hue, the impossible color of your mind. From this you conjure the Hollow Brain. The wisest among us have known the ritual for ages; how to open your interior so that it takes shape, stands before you and speaks. I can teach you. To print your nervous system on the air. To wander the dark alleys of your mind. If you can witness its secrets and remain intact… How much would you give, Jean, to speak with your subconscious?"

Jean bit her tongue against a scream – *stop saying my name!* If he were capable of believing this shit, about nervous systems and pupils and brains, she figured he was capable of anything. The company would trace the passenger if something happened, she assured herself; though maybe not without a complete profile. Maybe he didn't exist. *Soon enough,* she thought distantly, *neither will I.*

"I want you to remember where we've gone," the man said, voice grinding in her ears like a sink disposal. "Someone opened a corridor here many years ago. A more direct route into the wonders, as opposed to your inner eye. Come here if you feel lost." The passenger leaned forward; closer in the rearview, Jean saw how his skin drooped and hair quivered. "Stop here," he hushed.

She slammed on the brakes. The passenger kept himself upright through the shuddering halt. They had come to a field between the houses, covered in dead grass, the earth overturned and fallow at its center.

"Here?" she said. "What do you have to do here?"

"I'm visiting an old friend," said the passenger. He reached across the seat, past Jean's head. Her nerves spasmed so violently that she couldn't breathe. He tapped on the rearview three times, over the reflection of Jean's eyes. "Will you remember, Jean? Will you look?"

Before she could recover, tell him to get the fuck out, he glided from the backseat. His sharp knuckles rapped again on her window as he passed, and his cheeks writhed into a last smile.

He turned and waded into the grass, then bent himself over the circle of earth, pressed his hand against the soil, muttered a greeting, and waited for response. It seemed that one came as Jean drove away, swearing that she'd felt the earth tremble.

The passenger's words tapped at Jean's skull as she inched through traffic. The man was insane, she recognized, another person lost in their head, insisting that their madness had value. Still, she avoided her reflection, in case she saw something in her pupils – a wriggle of color, a flash of impossibility. For all its silliness, the idea wouldn't leave her.

This man had nothing, of course, on the people upstairs.

The fucking started early tonight. With each *thump* of the bedframe her body curled more tightly into itself. She stood on the mattress, feeling the vibrations through her palm, and thought of slamming her fist into the ceiling, shrieking every curse she knew at them. But what good would it do? They were still above her. She wanted no less than to look in their eyes as they went blank with terror. She wanted to feel them shrink and vanish, leaving only husks. Their bodies would rest well amongst these empty houses, where no one would think to look for them.

She didn't mean it, she assured herself, was just tired and fed up. People couldn't help but intrude on her space. Though she was no one, and had nothing, they insisted on worming their way inside.

Inside – yes, look inside. You know how to find it. The key to escape. The corridor to silence. He told you everything.

At the thought, her neurons flooded, a deluge of ideas and beliefs that weren't her own. The passenger's babbling echoed back to her, coherent and sure. He'd known a way to summon her soul in physical form – a way to know her deepest inner self. She remembered the terms the man had used, the Empty Hue and Hollow Brain. The names evoked images, like primal memory: a sea of nonsensical color, a writhing shape of veins or tendons, a perfect negative of her face. Though bizarre, their familiarity comforted her.

All it wants is to be recognized, the passenger's voice whispered. *Then it will give you anything.*

Someone screamed upstairs, not in terror but glee. The neighbors were breaking their record again.

Jean oozed from the bed, into the bathroom, and shut her door against the fucking. Her face stared from the mirror, twisted and puffy from interrupted sleep. She leaned toward the reflection, pulled her left eyelid down, and as the passenger had said, centered her vision on the pupils. She waited a moment, another. The fucking got louder, faster. Her pupil revealed nothing, just her reflection bent over the cornea. *What did you expect,* she thought, *your life is nothing, why wouldn't your inner self be nothing too?*

As despair moistened her eyes, as the fucking threatened to fracture her ceiling, she recognized it. The Empty Hue, flickering in the tunnel of her eye.

The molecules of her pupil shot out, a tide of non-matter, enveloping her in a tinted cyclone. For a moment she didn't exist except as a scream. Then she was drowning in a liquid tumor, dark as oil and thicker. When she stopped struggling, she felt herself borne aloft into matter that was vast and open, flickering with electric impulse.

~you~are~in~the~Empty~Hue~ the impulse said, its voice the texture of worms slithering through her brain. ~the~Empty~Hue~is~the~color~of~your~mind~

A pattern of reds, pinks, greens, tones that had no name danced through the atmosphere, in confirmation. *It speaks through colors,* she thought, and another pattern answered, zig-zagging like veins of light:

~you~see~it~as~color~~it~is~so~much~more~

In response she thought, *I want to know. Show me everything.*

The Hue split, and a line of shifting color fluttered out, violet ribbons widening in bursts. They curved and sloped like veins, not light or texture but sensation, graceful and savage in the way of tigers. She would have gasped in awe, had her lungs not stopped. This was cause for alarm, she knew, but she didn't care. Her inner space was gorgeous, immense, and total; she could stay there forever.

Fading into gentle green, the lines of Hue wrapped around each other and melted into an orb. It quivered, then sprouted a mass of hair-thin appendages, which twisted into limbs. As it drifted closer, the orb rippled and took on the shape of a head, Jean's head, but perfect and sure. In this place, there was nothing wrong with her.

All of this, her logic reminded, was a dream. Her heart heaved – in a moment she would open her eyes in her gray bed, her gray life, rotted out by gray anger. There was no color, no shape back there, only constant annoyance. Anguish gushed into her thoughts – the tendrils of the Hollow Brain responded, the purple of old blood.

It hears me, she thought in panic, and its surface flecked with red. *It feels me.* The Hue went soft again. *It understands me.* Its tendrils embraced her like a promise and its voice ran through her,

~acknowledge~the~interior~and~you'll~never~be~alone~again~

Against its undulations, she made her request.

The wish splattered against the Brain as a roiling yellow geyser, and its mirror-face pinched in disgust. She thought numbly, *I ruined it. It will destroy me for this.*

At the last word, the Hue ejected her back through her pupil, and she was awake, feet slamming to the floor, as two voices shrieked upstairs.

The sound vanished before Jean could fully hear it. She still felt the pressure of the Hue, the weight of her interior, the neon abyss that her body had become. She'd asked something of it, and it had responded. A quiet guilt prodded, *Go up, go see what you did.*

But as the pressure released and the room settled, she forgot what she'd seen, whether beautiful or awful, benign or malignant. There was only disappointment now and silence, into which she sank.

Jean woke to smothered midday light. Her body no longer felt corroded; her thoughts were no longer tinged with nightmares. She flung herself out of bed and opened the blinds. The crazy passenger's advice had worked. The day unfolded in a glittering display of potential, all the things she could do, all the things for which she'd lost the energy. Her mind lit up with to-do lists from months, a year prior. The apartment needed cleaning, errands needed running, there were things she had to *do,* all the accomplishments she would realize, not fantasies but occurrences, events, the result of effort and collaboration and –

Her attention turned abruptly upstairs. It sounded too quiet, like a large mass was keeping very still. She remembered her dream, the request she'd made, the horrible fate she'd wished upon the neighbors. The guilt prodded again, *You asked – it's your responsibility.*

Though Jean could dismiss it all as a nightmare, the guilt made too sharp a point. She grumbled and went into the hall. She'd never been to the other floors before, she realized; her nerves fritzed as she ascended the first step and froze. There were shoes on the landing.

Before Jean could duck away, the owner of the shoes scurried forward. He was a short man with plastered hair, nose drooping as if melted. The landlord, whom she hadn't seen since moving in. He stood outside the apartment above hers, the door half-open to perfect darkness.

He waved in dismissal. "No warning, no note," he hiccupped to himself.

Jean called back, "Is something wrong?"

His head darted like a turtle grabbing prey. "What's it to you?"

"I live under them," she snapped back.

He squinted, cataloging her face. "Bothersome tenants," he muttered, "always get what they deserve."

Jean hurried back to her room. The silence there was thick, almost tangible, like gums mashing together. Her throat closed and air wracked from her lungs. Her room felt contaminated. But if there was contamination, she thought, it had come from her, from her wish to the Empty Hue.

At the thought, she climbed onto her mattress, reached for the ceiling, and tapped three times. No one answered, no one was there. She knocked harder and called, "Hello?" Through the plaster came the emptiest sound, as if her apartment had been cut away from the building and dropped onto a tundra. Her veins froze at the idea of getting lost in that nothing.

Dropping onto the bed, Jean crawled under the sheets, crackling with dry sweat as she twisted and settled. She stared at the midday light out her window. Her goals withered as fast as they'd grown, her pleasant mood spoiled. This might be punishment, she considered, for all the times she'd imagined them dead. She'd never thought of herself as malicious – it was the callousness of *others* that inspired her fantasies – but maybe that was the justification they all gave, that *it's not them, it's* me *who was wronged.*

Jean sealed her eyes against the room, praying to the thing that wasn't there, to the Hollow Brain. *Take it back. I didn't mean it.* As she melted into early sleep, she did not hear a reply.

The air had the texture of a shower drain. Jean tasted it before she opened her eyes, crusted over with dried slime. She wiped them and swallowed, then retched. Everything was damp, her sheets, her hair, her skin, coated in fungal dust, spores of her anger. *This is a dream, just like before,* she told herself, even as she looked up.

The ceiling distended toward her like a corpse's belly. Green-black spores soaked through the plaster, threatening at any moment to split apart. Jean spat and choked, but only sucked in more filth. Her body felt malleable, soft. She tried to heave off the mattress – the substance pulled her back down. Bonded to the pillow, she couldn't turn away.

The plaster split and gorged ooze onto Jean's feet. She watched as the matter sputtered, then rose into a mound, flickering with sick red tones. She had seen this thing in her dream and found it beautiful. There was nothing beautiful about it now.

Like a candle melting in reverse, the substance built itself into a pillar. Its tendrils wound into each other and created two orbs, like human heads. The ooze slurped up and built into limbs, chests, abdomens. The forms were androgynous, the faces graceful. Though they had no teeth, they smiled.

Jean might have been afraid, but she knew what stood over her. Her Hollow Brain, returned from its errand, having fulfilled her wish. It looked like a nervous system ripped from the flesh and laid out, given its own life, still tender and uncertain of how to proceed. The non-matter of the Hue gushed from every appendage, an oil with no texture, only glints of color.

It must have crawled from her pupil while she dreamt, Jean tried to reason – crawled from her mind and into the upstairs apartment, where it swallowed her neighbors, absorbed, and became them. The shape of their bodies roiled with non-colors, rose-ochre-yellow-purple, in time with her shifting emotions. It seemed awful that they knew her this way – that she'd never be rid of them. They were inside her now.

In the voice of her thoughts, they began to speak; first in fragments, trying out language for the first time, then words:

~you~asked~the~wrong~thing~

"How was I supposed to know," she choked. It was insane to beg for help from her own mind. She'd birthed it, as the passenger said, and it had come out a monster.

~it's~not~too~late~

Jean couldn't protest as they gurgled toward her, hands interlocked. A bulge of rootlike arteries extended from their shared groin, horrid and fertile. It softened into another orb, a third head, much like her own. *What do you want from me?* she tried to say. Instead she leaned toward it, pressed her lips to the non-mouth. The material yielded and she sank inside. Her teeth, tongue and chin dissolved, and she thought of pain, but didn't feel any. It was almost a relief, knowing her body would not exist here, but inside the Empty Hue, forever conjoined with her Hollow Brain.

The Hue pushed into her throat, stomach, ribs, and organs, then crested over her head. The colors went dark, the ooze stopped writhing, her body stopped trembling, and her last thought hushed through the empty apartment,

~it's~quiet~

The City Archives

Paul L. Bates

THE RAT REMINDED Mitchel of a tomcat he once owned, or, at least, with whom he had shared his lodgings for a time several years ago. The rat was the same dark gray, easily as big as the cat, with that identical self-assured manner. It sat back on its haunches, unconcerned, as if sunbathing within the stark white swatch made by the streetlight's glare penetrating the tattered window shade, its eyes glinting like fathomless rubies.

"You again," Mitchel growled looking down from the bed. "I'm wide awake now, thanks to you. There's a baseball bat in the closet, especially for the uninvited. So, if you're still here when I get up, I'll make very short work of you, you may be sure of that."

The rat preened its whiskers for a moment to let Mitchel know it was not the least afraid, then turned slowly, sauntering into the darkness beyond, leaving Mitchel groping for the pull chain on the flimsy table lamp beside the bed, wondering the location of the rat hole. With a click, the dreary room took on a warm glow. The soft light effused across the mound of grubby blankets, the rusted chrome legged table in the corner with its single matching chair, the threadbare carpet and the old leather sofa that looked as if it were about to heave one last sigh before slouching into itself forever. The rat was gone, as usual. Its means of entry still a mystery. Had he dreamed their encounter again?

Mitchel got up, went through the uninspired ritual that comprised his work-week mornings, before trudging into the dreary day without.

On the street traffic crawled, honked, assumed an acutely threatening air. Mitchel stayed on the sidewalk, pausing only to sip through the hole in the plastic lid of the large coffee from the corner convenience store, stealing glances at those few other bundled souls scurrying through the cold dark at this ridiculous hour.

The underground entry was only a block away, an uninviting burrow with a gag-worthy reek, and a filthy fiberglass awning above the steep stairway down. The straining overhead lights within the station barely glinted on the cold steel rails and all but denied the presence of a ceiling lurking somewhere in the spreading gloom above. The once bright walls were speckled with small white tiles—a mosaic fog bank, cracked and yellowed with age. Uniformly mildewed grout and a subtle rippling made the entire surface look as if it were gradually buckling inward bespeaking the inevitable collapse of the stations, the tunnels, the city over time.

A sorry assemblage of featureless, immobile figures exuded an almost tangible indifference. They shivered, clung to their overcoats, sucked on lidded coffee cups, studied their shoes, clutching folded newspapers, with an assortment of battered lunch pails and scruffy briefcases at their feet, waiting for the always overdue train. Each kept as much distance between themselves and the next rider as possible. The atmosphere was thick, tasted of filth, a lingering scent of regurgitated canned stew. Somehow all of it completely distorted Mitchel's sense of time passing in a most dreamlike manner until, at long last, he heard his train screeching in the dark distance, announcing itself from within the gaping void.

Mitchel felt himself pressed into the curved plastic seat as the train lurched through the labyrinth of tunnels, its faint rows of thin overhead lights blinking erratically, often plunging the compartment into absolute darkness. To Mitchel, this prolonged gloom was like those long-drawn-out moments when falling asleep, waiting for the night's first mindless dream to congeal from the final collapse of the day's last meandering thought.

The protracted darkness sparked a misplaced memory of a nightmare that had eluded him in the presence of the rat. A man in a dark gray raincoat whose face Mitchel could not recall had handed him a short-barreled revolver, pointed emphatically in the direction of a stately three-story sandstone home surrounded by a high stucco wall, in some fashionable neighborhood on the outskirts of the city. Mitchel was certain the building had not been part of the dream moments before. The man had vanished when Mitchel turned to study the meticulous façade. Alone, Mitchel had opened the pistol's cylinder, inspected its lethal contents, making certain that all six chambers were loaded, disengaged the trigger safety, slogged toward the building with as much enthusiasm as he typically felt going to work. The detailed dream memory to this point was as remarkably tactile as it was visual.

He did not recall entering or navigating the enormous house, only standing at the foot of a massive black bed in which a barrel-chested gray-haired man slept fitfully beside his slender wife beneath crimson silk sheets and a matching quilt. They lay back-to-back, as far from one another as possible, leaving a space large enough for Mitchel to lie down comfortably between them. *An odd coupling,* he had thought, as the man looked to be at least twice the age and size of the woman. He studied the wife's pale expressionless face. Her shoulder length blond hair retained its unnatural sweep behind her head even while she slept, as if held in place by lacquer. Her hair and posture suggested a bored and lonely sentry stationed at some remote outpost diligently guarding something utterly inconsequential, unlikely to ever be stolen. The man, on the other hand, squirmed as if plagued by a merciless demon, clutched his bedclothes, twisted his immaculate red silk pajamas as he struggled to find relief from his tortured dreams.

Mitchel had watched impassively until the man awoke, sat up, stared into Mitchel's unblinking eyes, worked his mouth as if to speak, finding no words whatever to stay Mitchel's hand. One perfect shot, between the eyes; a noise like a thunderclap against a mountainside that made his ears ring; that unmistakable corrosive fragrance of cordite. The big man fell back into the waiting embrace of the fluffy red pillows, his body gone rigid like stone, eyes wide and uncomprehending, a dark hole trickling blood in his brow. The woman did not move save to smile slightly in her sleep. A frozen moment that seemed to last much too long; then the abrupt blackness, not unlike riding the underground when the grime covered yellow strip lights flicker for long torturous moments at a time.

 A bitterly cold drizzle began to fall just as Mitchel stepped cautiously onto the sidewalk again. The City Archives was only a block from the underground. The merest suggestion of dawn silhouetted the city's stark towers, cast an ethereal sheen upon the cracked and heaving pavement. Mindful of the thin ice frosting, Mitchel climbed the worn steel tipped steps that narrowed as they rose to the colossal brick archway. The beefy old security guard stationed miserably within the gloomy portico aimed his flashlight into Mitchel's face, studying the young man's squinting features as if the weekend had once again obliterated his memory of the staff. The guard eventually grunted his recognition, allowing Mitchel to enter the sacred citadel of recorded information. Mitchel grunted back. Inside, Mitchel slogged forward in the semidarkness toward the basement stairs at the rear of the building listening to the crisp echoes of his plodding footfalls down the endless gaping corridors, still frigid while the rumbling furnace below struggled to its task.

 Mitchel was early, as usual; punched his timecard, hung his overcoat, scarf and hat in the first of five battered lockers nestled within the shallow niche beside the clock. Two of the four overhead fluorescent fixtures remained broken. The other two struggled with mismatched sputtering bulbs, buzzing like bothersome insects. At his desk within the vault, he ate the swirled sugar covered pastry he had bought with the thin coffee, as always noting it tasted less like cinnamon and more like what he imagined the flavor of cardboard to be.

 The mountain of rolled drawings he sorted had again miraculously grown taller; a phenomenon Mitchel had more than once been tempted to document. He had not done so because the practicality of the job security it offered him slightly outweighed his mounting curiosity. His supervisor had assured him that his position at the City Archives was temporary; that the drawings he was sorting and filing had all been drawn between the years 1920 and 1940, and therefore could not possibly have multiplied. Those drawn before and those drawn after were being sorted and filed by other clerks in similar vaults. Mitchel had simply assumed the other four timecards, the other four lockers corroborated this fact, even though he had never actually met, seen, or heard anyone else working in the basement Archives.

Standing on an old wooden stepladder, Mitchel selected six heavy rolls from the top of the pile that extended across the entire north side of the room on a series of old pine slat pallets. The stack rose intermittently from five to six feet, an abstraction of an ocean's wave approximating a paper tide. He opened the rolls one at a time, turning his head away to avoid the inevitable cloud of fine dust and mildew that arose, hovered like a shallow fog, fell back onto the documents in a dry rain. He brushed away the broken bits of paper at the crumbling tattered corners, waiting for the occasional startled silverfish disrupted in mid-meal to relocate. The drawings gave the vault a unique mustiness, a smell and feel of raw entropy, an indisputable firsthand experience of all things winding down, decaying, atrophying, dying, disintegrating—a perfect metaphor for a seemingly pointless existence.

Mitchel then separated the drawings by category—conceptual design, site work, architectural, structural, mechanical—spreading them on the two ancient, massive, slightly uneven white oak conference tables set end to end relegated to the task. He covered the open drawings with large sheets of thick cardboard on which he placed a dozen or so battered bricks in a halfhearted attempt to encourage the velum to lose its comfortable memory of having been rolled for so long. He then located the appropriate flat files in which to store them, arranged by address—north to south, east to west—examined the space available within the designated drawers. These spaces were more often than not much too small, too close to the drawings of the next building which entailed his rearranging the existing files to accommodate the newer ones almost every time he added another set, necessitating his relabeling nearly everything that followed. More pointless, uninspired, time-consuming tasks to be filed under the dubious heading of job security.

Occasionally, he would find drawings within the files of buildings he knew had been demolished. These he would mark, reroll, relocate to a small pallet near the door. Someone inevitably filed these in another section of the City Archives as their value was now purely historical. Who did this or when remained another mystery, as the drawings always disappeared whenever Mitchel was absent from the vault.

His supervisor, Mr. Moriarty, had once sat silently at Mitchel's desk watching him working for over an hour. "You're the best yet," Mr. Moriarty had concluded before leaving. "Methodical, not easily distracted, with the requisite respect for the documents you handle. You will go far, Mitchel—trust me, you *will* go far."

He rarely saw Mr. Moriarty, perhaps no more than once a month, usually a chance meeting at the somber employee's automat cafeteria which was typically otherwise empty. Mr. Moriarty would stop briefly at the small table where Mitchel ate alone, place a fatherly hand firmly upon Mitchel's shoulder, mouth some rambling disingenuous inanity about the importance of the work Mitchel was doing, exhort him to maintain his good efforts, intimate that better things lay ahead.

It was during one of these impromptu encounters that Mitchel had mentioned that over the past year the rolled drawing pile had seemingly grown in spite of his best efforts to diminish it. Moriarty had withdrawn his hand at once. He scowled, studying Mitchel as an exterminator might examine a dead cockroach, looking for aberrant mutations with an icy professional curiosity, before sweeping it away. It was the only time his supervisor had ever expressed any displeasure at his accomplishments. Mitchel never made mention of the offending observation again.

So, it came as a complete surprise to Mitchel when he climbed down from the step ladder with his next armload of drawings, that Mr. Moriarty stood patiently beside his desk, clad, as usual, in a spotless gray raincoat, clutching his ubiquitous businessman's black folding umbrella, his small moustache twitching sporadically.

"I didn't hear you enter, sir," Mitchel said, laying the large rolls carefully on the oak tables with as little noise as possible.

"It's a terrible thing," Mr. Moriarty began, subtly shaking his head. "Mr. Wickersham, who, as you may know, for many years ran the City Archives, unexpectedly died in his sleep last night. It was he who felt these venerable drawings you file rated this special care, prior to their being electronically recorded. It was he who thought there was some historical significance to this soon-to-be lost art of hand drafting—a respect not shared by his contemporaries, I'm afraid. Now, with his passing, and the city-wide austerity program being implemented by the new administration, all those, such as yourself, who were hired strictly on a temporary basis to perform this task, will, in all probability, be summarily dismissed."

"Right now?" was all that Mitchel could think of asking.

A rare spontaneous smile briefly softened Mr. Moriarty's usually austere countenance. "No, no, my boy. Not for some little while yet, I imagine; although how small a while I would not venture to guess. Mr. Wickersham's replacement has not been designated, but will be shortly, I'm quite certain. I'm here simply as a courtesy to warn you, so that when your position, such as it is, is terminated, as it inevitably will be, the whole sad business comes as no shock to you and is, therefore, much less awkward for me."

With that, Mr. Moriarty adopted what Mitchel took to be his typical attempt at a fleeting fatherly grimace, gripped his umbrella tighter, bade Mitchel get on with his sorting. Mitchel watched Moriarty open the vault door, where he vacillated, most theatrically, pausing to reflect for a moment, safe within the shadows.

"You know, Mitchel," Moriarty intoned, choosing each word with pronounced care, "it would be an appropriate gesture on your part, for you to attend the funeral. Arrangements haven't been made yet, to be sure, but I imagine it will take place before week's end. It is exactly the sort of thing a young man *with prospects* would do. I'll inform you when and where."

The days of the week followed one another in their usual unrelentingly dreary succession, the only event to mark any one of them was the appearance on Mitchel's desk of a small off-white card with a handwritten note stating *funeral*, giving the time and place, with a quick afterthought scrawled beneath it, *dress appropriately*. Moriarty's warning gave him exactly one day's notice, leaving him to wonder what within the drab sameness of his small wardrobe would be *appropriate* for Wickersham's funeral. The weather, too, had remained stubbornly relentless for the entire week, punctuated by a persistent light rain that more often than not froze into a treacherous glaze upon the weary gray streets and sidewalks slowing the already sluggish traffic to a near standstill until the lumbering sanders counteracted its effects. As much in deference to the weather as to his supervisor, Mitchel bought a more affordable version of the businessman's black folding umbrella that Moriarty carried.

The cemetery memorial service was even more depressing than Mitchel had expected. All attention was riveted upon a monstrously stout archbishop with a quivering lower lip who spoke languidly and loudly, modulating his voice unnecessarily, as if to keep his bored parishioners awake. The man enumerated without letup all of the inestimable achievements, both personal and civic, of the late and much-lamented Mr. Clive Wickersham. The booming nasal voice easily pierced the thick crowd of black umbrellas, grey raincoats, the remorseless patter of the taunting rain, the metallic whine of the occasional passing bus or funeral procession, even hammering down the usual shield of introspection Mitchel maintained around himself.

He stood on the periphery of the gathering, atop a small knoll, looking down upon the distant well-fed clergyman, the petite blond woman in the black veil at his side, the troop of officious pallbearers and those intimidating figures gripping voluminous black umbrellas, keeping the relentless drizzle from disrupting the solemnity of the occasion for those officiating, all posed somberly around the colossal black casket like a troop of distraught vultures.

Mitchel spotted Moriarty within the field of undulating umbrellas, halfway between himself and the open grave, but only momentarily. Moriarty was too far away to either acknowledge or approach. Mitchel was acquainted with no one else present, was introduced to no one, went back to work late in the afternoon wondering why he had attended the tedious function at all, and whose eyes in that otherwise staid gathering had repeatedly searched his features, whenever he had looked away, only to avert themselves whenever he sought them out in turn.

Half an hour before the end of the workweek, Moriarty appeared at his desk to formally discharge him. The supervisor made no mention of the fact that he had seen Mitchel at the funeral or why Mitchel's position was being terminated. He handed Mitchel his final paycheck—which contained no formal severance pay but which did include his vacation wages through the end of the following week without deducting time spent at the funeral—then bade him clean out his locker.

The icy rain had let up a bit when Mitchel emerged from the City Archives for the last time. Calculating how much of his meager salary he had saved over the past two years and how long it would last him if he were frugal, he decided to forgo the underground, walk the twelve blocks to his apartment. He arrived tired and hungry, his old tan raincoat drenched through, just as the darkening, immobile cloud bank that had for so long lingered oppressively above the city broke at long last, in time to reveal a blood red sunset.

Mitchel was surprised to see a large black limousine idling before the building's front entrance, a fog of toxic vapor hovering at its rear. It was hardly the sort of vehicle one would expect to find in this neighborhood. Its windows were tinted a dark bronze, revealing nothing save his own haggard features staring quizzically back at him as he trudged past.

Once within the relative comfort of his apartment, he struggled out of his soggy clothes, stuffed them in the overflowing hamper, took a long hot shower. He was too numb and tired from the cold walk to further contemplate his dire financial predicament.

His wet hair very much disheveled, the shabby towel wrapped tight around his waist, Mitchel filled the teakettle, placed it on a burner, rummaged about the tiny alcove that passed for a kitchen looking for the tin of sugar and a teabag, scooping the one and dropping the other into a chipped and stained white mug. A sharp rapping on his apartment door gave him a start. He thought to at least put on his trousers before answering, but another insistent banging hard upon the heels of the first convinced him otherwise.

He opened the door to be nearly trampled by a petite blond woman in a stylish black wool dress and veil who barged into his private squalor radiating an anger so intense it made him wince. She surveyed the small room with unbridled disgust, looked Mitchel up and down, noted his obvious discomfort, made a calculatingly cold smile, that somehow pierced her veil.

"You killed my husband," she announced in a steady quiet voice.

Mitchel, who by that time had recognized her as both the woman at the funeral by her dress and posture, as well as the woman from his dream earlier in the week by her impassive face and impeccable hood of blond hair, stood speechless. Of what possible use would it be to say it had all been a dream? He shut the door behind her instead.

"Moriarty assures me," the woman continued unperturbed, "that you are a young man with prospects."

Again, Mitchel found nothing whatever to reply. Of what use would it be to confide that at the moment he had neither job, significant assets nor any foreseeable prospects whatsoever?

"And," she added, "you appear to be a man who knows when to keep his mouth shut in the presence of a woman. That, too, is commendable."

The teakettle began its unrelenting whistling, rattling on the stove. Mitchel hurriedly turned away to shut off the burner. He waved at the mug offering the woman some tea.

"Don't be ridiculous," she snapped, a disapproving scowl briefly distorting her otherwise placid features. She shot a quick look around the room, as if by way of elucidation.

Mitchel just nodded, poured the boiling water into the mug, gathered up some dry clothes, went back into the humid, claustrophobic bathroom to brush his hair, shave, and dress himself as quickly as he could, taking the tea with him.

When he emerged, the woman was standing in the open doorway, one foot planted firmly in the common corridor without.

"I need a handyman," she said matter-of-factly. "Can you manage tools?"

"Of course," Mitchel spoke at last, doing his utmost to sound credible.

"Good. It doesn't pay well, but room and board are included. Leave your other things behind. I'll replace everything with something more suitable. But do bring your umbrella." She turned to go, then added, almost as an afterthought, "From time to time, I'll require other services from you—do you understand?"

Mitchel nodded, not at all confident that he really did understand anything, but certain nonetheless that as a young man with prospects he must never display hesitation, never admit ignorance; equally certain he would catch on to everything, all in good time.

These Graceless, Grasping Hands

Dyani Sabin

please, the mouse prays, beneath the owl's
talons, *i need
a miracle*

god, the owl cries, one dinner
between it and starvation
just one miracle.

the family gathers around
the dying
please
they beg
please.

I cannot tell them this,

as the beloved slips into death—
gracefully—

but,

there are many
kinds of
miracles

The Flytrap Garden

Perry Ruhland

How can the fancies of a starved mind be expected to compete with a total, smothering gray? They couldn't. I understood that the only real counter to reality was another, more potent reality.

This is how I came to frequent that great expanse of forest that rimmed the lower edge of town. It seemed to me that the gray dullness that had been all-pervasive within the borders could not quite contaminate these woods. The cluster of sagging trees and rolling hills was hardly Arcadia, but it provided ample escape.

It was the equinox of an unusually vibrant autumn, a day when the sun shone bright behind shattered clouds; when the trees flashed blades of red, gold, and purple; when everything shivered as if in anticipation of the year's fast-approaching terminus. I had skipped school (hardly a new development) and been wandering for some hours now, mind lost in the folds of the leafy quilt overhead, until I tripped on a fallen branch. Without realizing, I stumbled upon the remains of some long-neglected path. I followed the path down a winding hill and across a bubbling stream, and in time I came to a canyon rich with decay. Years later, after the avalanche, I would learn this canyon had been used to house a fledgling industrial district, but a freak fire struck the development down in its infancy, reducing the buildings to a network of low walls and tilted columns that resembled Roman ruins. A single construct survived: a soda manufacturing plant that was shuttered after only a month of operation. Years of neglect had taken an obvious toll on the factory, and while the inferno may have spared the structure, time proved far less merciful. The rightmost foundations of the building gave out long ago, and the entire right half had deflated into a collapse of brick and steel, giving its silhouette the appearance of a sagging shoulder. A mesh of red-leafed veins scaled the fragmentary slope, creeping up past stout smokestacks and encroaching on the gables of the vaulted glass ceiling. The ruin loomed over the razed canyon and acted as her iron tombstone, a bloated corpse whose ongoing putrescence served as a totem for the land's decrepit soul.

I wondered then if death and decay could enchant even the grayest of things.

One of the factory's doors was cracked open. A sickly sweetness emanated from the dark, a heavy scent reminiscent of overripe fruit and fermenting breads. I found myself lost in a black sea that allowed only the occasional islands, irregular patches of filtered sunlight that shone in from broken windows to illuminate not just the sheet metal archipelagos and rebar shipwrecks, but the coral reefs of empty bottles, the oil spills of blood-dark cola, the school of glass-shard jellyfish that blinkered in the lacquered depths. The high ceiling was largely engulfed by darkness, but I could make out the odd vine dipping down from the humid shadow: fat, leafy tendrils, reeking of sour bile.

Their stench was nothing compared to the odor that radiated from deep within the factory, that same sickly sweetness. In lieu of any lighted path, I followed this odor down winding halls thick with shadow, sweltering tunnels enclosed in obscure foliage, emerging only briefly in lit slivers of decay.

I cannot say how long I wandered, just that when I reached that aching heart I was exhausted, and the humidity had left me sweating, thirsty, and weak. I emerged from the dark into what I assume was once a foreman's office, an elevated box that overlooked the factory floor. The vaulted glass ceiling hung above like the gabled peak of a chapel, a cross-hatched atrium permitting the soft light of a premature autumn dusk. Beneath that melancholy glow, the contents of the office were displayed clearly: they held no shortage of the wonder that had been all-but vanquished from my town. The office was crowded with tables stacked with all sorts of dusty glassware, largely mason jars and refurbished cola bottles. Some receptacles housed murky fluids or densely packed earth, but the majority were home to strange specimens, insects that could have only been plucked from dreams. Among the fantastic ranks were thimble-shaped dragonflies and fleur-de-lis spiders, pill bugs that curled into jagged-tooth pyramids, cicadas sporting vivid constellations on black sky carapaces, and a whole colony of varicolored ants which, having been confined to a disused cola bottle, resembled the rainbow-hued shards of a kaleidoscope.

On the walls, the expected workplace missives and inspirational photos were absent, and the chipped tile surfaces were all but smothered by a ream of bizarre charts. These charts were composed on yellowed parchment, their diagrams sketched in thick blotted ink, and although they lacked any cohesive subject, they were all clearly drawn by the same flamboyant, imprecise hand. Some held obvious relevance: insectoid reproductive cycles, paths of burrowed colonies, stages of chrysalis, the makeup of certain carnivorous plants, and assorted anatomical charts of a miscellany of winged insects; but many more were noticeably broader in scope, including complex food chains that charted a legacy of consumption from hazy microbes to cold-eyed humans, and even elaborate ringed cosmologies wherein an oblate Earth, and in some examples, the entirety of the spiraling Milky Way, barely registered as a black speck against a parchment universe. Stranger still were the few works that, despite lurking among these stylized diagrams, seemed to belong to a wholly different genus. Here, the artist seemed to disregard the studied compositions of their earlier scientific works to embrace a sort of hieroglyphic symbolism, where simple shapes illustrated abstract scenes. In these works, radiant spheres hung perilously in the gaping maws of blotted shadows that dominated the canvas. Some of these spheres had wings, some had placid faces, some were marked with the craters of moons and others the unfamiliar continents of distant planets. The shadows — hungry, jagged things — were the same in each.

I had become so caught up in admiring the specimens and illustrations that, for a while, I had neglected the most obvious fixture of the room: the large, shattered window that overlooked the factory floor. As soon as I registered it, the rest of the trip came flooding back to me; the heat, the sweat, and of course that awful stench, now a full, sharp thing, an all-consuming miasma that clouded the room and fumed directly into my nostrils. The shock of the scent, and the strength of its return, was enough to double me over; I shuffled to the window with failing strength and peered forth to find just what horrible thing had polluted this crumbling husk.

The industrial space had been almost wholly reclaimed by nature. Sick, hateful flora writhed across the walls, flowers wept. Conveyor belts — thick, snakelike tracks that once ran lengthwise across the floor like pews — were now gutted, their husks warped into planters for a garden sown in the depths of a frenzied imagination.

The garden was composed entirely of flytraps. Even in their ordinary forms, those frightful predators are the most alien of all earthly flora, but evidently their gardener was not satisfied by such mundane horrors. Instead he had chosen to cultivate breeds of flytraps beyond the limits natural horticulture would allow: azure flytraps whose maws hinged loose from spiraling stems, flytraps with jaws of jagged shark teeth, large-mouthed flytraps whose pink gullet could easily fit a human's hand, or perhaps a small child's head. The plants were clearly well-fed, as their hulking flowers drooped in full bloom, suspended fireworks of radiant color. All of the plants' jaws were open, and from their maws fumed that sickly sweetness — a siren song which had doubtlessly lured innumerable desperate insects to their doom.

The Flytrap Garden

In the center of the garden rose an elevated platform, a tarnished moon with a waist-high rail. The platform, like the conveyor belts, surely served some industrial purpose before but was now transformed into a crude chancel. The back half of the platform was devoted to a large, makeshift altar constructed from wooden tables that housed a variety of glassware, each filled with insects of the same fantastical stock that were housed in the office. On the other side of the altar rose a spindly metal lectern on which rested a large, black book. The lectern faced the office, and even with the view height afforded me, I could not see the pages. Not that I was particularly interested anyways, for between the altar and the lectern, a stranger was waiting. It was an elderly man, stout and vaguely toadstool shaped, with a tumorous head wholly free of hair. He was kneeling before the lectern, his tattered brown robes swallowing his knees, his head bowed. I could not discern any facial features. He knelt there unmoving; at first I wondered if he was sleeping, then I wondered if he was dead. It was only after considering his monastic appearance that I realized the man was likely in meditation, lost in some inward trance beneath the setting sun. I strained my ears, listened for murmured prayer. I heard only the rhythm of my breath, and the rush of my blood, and a distant buzzing.

The monk rose. His mirrored head struck a blade of sunlight and, for a moment, cast a flare. Beneath the golden glow, he turned from the lectern and began to shuffle towards the altar, his cut pace and trailing robe reminded me of a snail. Upon reaching the altar he bowed gently, retrieving a soda bottle packed with obscure insects. He lifted the specimen up to the light to inspect it, and I saw, for the first time, the details of his face — his sunken black-pit eyes, his cinderblock nose, and the lipless line of his mouth which folded up slowly into a smile.

The monk admired the bottle for a moment more. Then, with his little square fingers, he yanked off the lid and shook the vessel ferociously.

From the glass confines flew a cloud of screaming insects; desperate, hungry things rudely awakened from their deathlike sleep. Like a bursting fountain the bugs shot up and dispersed through the black church, flying blind towards their surrounding sweetness, soaring down to their fate. Soon these bugs were joined by other doomed souls, and before I could register what was happening the room descended into chaos. I did not dare divert my gaze as I watched those marvels, the miracle spawn of dreams, fly eagerly to their deaths. For I could see it now in precise detail, every moment, every atom registered clearly and fully as if my eyes were those of God. I would not miss a moment of it, not a triggered hair, not a snuffed light, not one single twitch of a small dying limb. I could no longer hear the rhythm of my breath nor the rush of my blood, and though I must have screamed, it was lost beneath the symphony of buzzing wings and snapping jaws. In the center of that awful vortex, I saw the monk, the gardener, the conductor, the creator. I saw him see me. Then it was dark.

I awoke in the morning on the road to our town, dehydrated but otherwise unharmed. The adults in town seemed nonplussed by my state and chalked my tale up to nothing more than the delirium of a fever-stricken child. After a week of restless nightmares, I decided it was best to agree with them; it was not as if there weren't other things I had to focus on. School, for example, with its ochre uniforms and jagged desks, possessed a certain allure I had never before appreciated, and when the time came to graduate into the lofty position of market clerk, I was more than happy to embrace the tedium. The days were dull, and I was thankful.

It was some years later when an earthquake struck the countryside. According to reports, this triggered the avalanche which buried the long-forgotten canyon, wiping the former industrial district from the Earth. My coworkers and I gossiped of the event over our brief lunches, and we all agreed it was excellent that we had nothing like those blasted ruins here. I said something rather stupid about a vengeful Earth, like some great beast, opening its jaws to swallow the aberration. Nobody cared too much for that.

Every morning I tell myself that my life has generally been one of great comfort and minimal distress. A house, a job, a wife, two kids. I spend my nights sitting with a drink and basking in the comfortable silence that rattles in my head. Despite it all, there is something that still bothers me. It's a dream, a cruelty ensnaring me when I least expect it. In this dream, I stand atop an elevated platform in a deserted factory, an altar to my left and a lectern to my right. Above me, a vaulted glass ceiling reveals a black carapace rich with constellations, brighter than I have ever known. An old man stands beside me. His lipless mouth curls into a smile and wrapped in tattered robes he offers me his hand.

And so we dance, the creator and I, across the chancel and beneath twinkling stars, to the music of a feasting garden, a song of wonder and terror indivisible. When I awake, my pillow is wet, and I pretend I don't know why.

THE PLACE, THE PEOPLE, THE PREDATORS: THE LIGOTTIAN WORLD OF VANCOUVER'S DOWNTOWN EASTSIDE

Shawn Phelps

Like Dr. Locrian's asylum, Vancouver's Downtown Eastside is a place where madness is allowed to "breathe with a life of its own." The neighborhood's residents have been put "through a battery of hellish ordeals," which serve to "loosen their attachment to the world of humanity and to project them further into the absolute, the realm of the silent staring universe." But unlike Thomas Ligotti's fictional asylum, the nightmare world of the Downtown Eastside is very real. It is a place where the mad roam freely, addicts seek forbidden pleasures, and people disappear.

The Place

"He talked about a place that sounded like the back alleys of some cosmic slum, an interdimensional dead end."
—"The Frolic" by Thomas Ligotti.

Vancouvers' Downtown Eastside is a place where Ligotti's character, Jon Doe, might have brought his young playmates for a "frolic." Doe might have been describing this neighborhood when he spoke of the "black-foaming gutters and back alleys," where he carried out his murderous agenda. The rain-soaked environment of Vancouver's skid row is very much like "the dank windowless gloom of some galactic cellar."[1]

In December 2006, the *Vancouver Sun* called the Downtown Eastside "our four blocks of hell." The *Sun* described it as an area "so filthy and hazardous that sanitation workers have asked for police protection." It is a netherworld with "human feces and urine polluted lanes, sex-trade detritus littered public areas, and buildings opened up to vermin." Despite an annual government expenditure of around $360 million, the area seems resistant to rehabilitation. Several intensive management projects have failed and the "area reverted to baseline conditions within three to four days."[2]

The concentration of poverty, mental illness, and drug abuse in this small neighborhood make it unique in North America. Its streets are populated by gibbering schizophrenics, who caper and rant. Crystal methamphetamine addicts barrel through the crowds, racing to destinations unknown even to themselves. Stony-eyed groups of aboriginals, faces like baked brick, glare with silent menace at passersby. Mini skirt wearing sex workers, legs covered in oozing sores, hustle for business. Everywhere people are openly injecting drugs.

Sudden violence erupts and just as quickly fades. The participants often seem puzzled as to the cause of their conflict. They stagger away on sidewalks that are a Jackson Pollack composition of bird droppings, vomit, syringes, condoms, mucus, cigarette butts, and trash. Pigeons strut and nod knowingly, perhaps reading some occult meaning in the swirling patterns of refuse.

Local churches provide food and shelter to some, but religious services are poorly attended. The idea of a loving deity seems laughable under these circumstances. Perhaps an Old Testament Yahweh demanding blood sacrifices would be more appropriate.

---

[1] Thomas Ligotti, *Songs of a Dead Dreamer*, 18.

[2] Janet Steffenhagen, "Our Four Blocks of Hell," *Vancouver Sun*, December 8, 2006.

The People

"We were kept alive in some form, any form, as long as we were viciously thrashing about, acting out of the most intensely vital impulses, never allowed to become still and silent until every drop had been drained of the blackness flowing inside us."[3]

To walk through the Downtown Eastside is to enter a sideshow displaying every permutation of aberrant human behavior. "Thousands of psychiatric patients from hospitals such as Coquitlam's Essondale and Riverview were deinstitutionalized by provincial governments in the 1970's. The Downtown Eastside was the only place where they could afford to live and where they felt welcome."[4]

During the Great Depression an influx of unemployed people came to Vancouver seeking work. The region's mild climate made it a destination for the poor and homeless. Unlike the rest of Canada, it was possible to spend the winter living on the streets without freezing to death.

The availability of cocaine, fentanyl, heroin, and crystal methamphetamine in the neighborhood make it a mecca for substance abusers. Despite efforts by the police, the port of Vancouver is a clearinghouse for drugs coming from Asia and South America, which are then openly traded on the streets of the Downtown Eastside.

Every person in the neighborhood has their own story, a unique chain of events that led them to the neighborhood. But doctors, nurses, and social workers have discovered something many of them have in common: a history of "nearly inconceivable trauma" as children. Many Downtown Eastside residents "suffered severe neglect and maltreatment in childhood. Almost all the addicted women inhabiting the area were sexually assaulted in childhood; as

---

[3] Thomas Ligotti. My Work is Not Yet Done, 112.

[4] Steve Cameron, "*On the Farm*," Vintage Canada 2011. 56-57.

were many of the men... residents tell stories of pain upon pain: rape, beatings, humiliation, rejection, abandonment, and relentless character assassination."[5]

Amid this poverty, drug, and mental illness fueled chaos, the government attempts to maintain order. An army of doctors, nurses, social workers, police, paramedics, and firemen work to combat this humanitarian disaster, but any thought of victory has long been abandoned; all that is hoped for is containment. There came a dawning realization that these people were too damaged to be "cured." Instead, a new treatment modality, *harm reduction*, was instituted. It would only seek to mitigate the damage addicts did to themselves and society.

In early 2020, a type of narcotic vending machine was introduced in the Downtown Eastside. In this program, "registered opioid users, who have been evaluated on their drug use, health status and social situation, are prescribed a heroin-alternative called hydromorphone which they receive on a predetermined schedule." The machine, "an 800-pound secure dispenser similar to an ATM, is located near the Overdose Prevention site on East Hastings Street. It uses a biometric scanner that reads the vein pattern on the palm of a user's hand to verify their identity.[6]

Perhaps curing these troubled people of their addictions should not be a treatment objective. Otto Rank, one of Freud's early disciples, described the dilemma commenting that "it is not so much a question as to whether we are able to cure a patient, whether we can or not, *but whether we should or not.*"[7] Should individuals who had been subjected to lifetimes of horror be deprived of the one means of relief at their disposal? Instead, perhaps physicians should be giving out narcotics in whatever quantity is needed to ease the

---

[5] Gabor Mate MD. *In the Land of the Hungry Ghosts. Close Encounters with Addiction*. Vintage Canada, 2012. 62.

[6] Simon Little, "Worlds First Biometric Opioid Vending Machine." *Global News*, January 17, 2020.

[7] Otto Rank, Quoted in *The Denial of Death*. Becker, Ernest. The Free Press, 2001. 270.

overwhelming psychic agony of their patients. This would be rather like the palliative, or hospice, approach used in terminal cancer patients.

For even in sleep, there is no relief as many suffer horrifying nightmares, reliving past traumas night after night, entering dreamscapes so hellish they will go to any length to avoid sleep. Residents describe using crystal methamphetamine solely for the purpose of avoiding sleep and the visions it brings. Others seek oblivion through heroin and other narcotics. These substances are used "in order to avoid trauma reminders, or distressing reexperiencing symptoms including intrusive memories, nightmares, and flashbacks. Sedation is desired in the hope that nightmares might be avoided."[8]

Dr. Gabor Mate, a Vancouver addictions expert, described the experiences of one of his patients:

Celia recalls being sexually exploited for the first time at the age of five, by her stepfather. "It went on for eight years. Recently I've been reliving the abuse in my dreams." In her nightmares, Celia is drenched in her stepfather's saliva. "That was a ritual," she explains with an almost flat matter-of-factness. "When I was a little girl, he would stand over my bed and spit all over me."[9] Stories like Celia's are the norm among DTES residents.

The Predators

"The machinery of my murderous rage was grinding its gears, burning its oil into toxic vapors, shooting out sparks right and left, shooting and shooting until the mirror before me began to glow with an eerie incandescence. There it was, at the center of that infernal aura. There was my face, radiant with

---

[8] David Cooper, *Practice in Mental Health-Substance Abuse.* Radcliffe Publishing Ltd, 2011.

[9] Gabor Mate MD, *In the Land of the Hungry Ghosts. Close Encounters with Addiction.* Vintage Canada 2012. 62.

obsessive hate. There were my eyes, pitching daggers from behind amber tinted lenses. There I stood in the full blackness of my form."[10]

British Columbia as a whole has twice the national rate of missing persons. Many of the missing are women who resided in the Downtown Eastside. Explanations for these disappearances remain elusive. Some feel that the unique environment of the region has some deleterious effect on the human psyche.

"It could be the rain. It could be the salt air corroding the brain synapses that keep extreme antisocial behavior in check. It could be the sheer enormity and imposing dignity of some of the grandfather trees that anchor the Pacific Northwest to the rest of the continent, but the area seems to attract or grow more than its fair share of serial killers, mostly preying on vulnerable women."[11]

Robert "Willy" Pickton grew up on a farm in Port Coquitlam, 17 miles east of Vancouver. The Pickton family farm was mostly "below the water table, which meant acres of brackish, swampy land as well as patches of dangerous quicksand on the Eastern side. A foul lagoon took up space near the back."[12] A 600lb boar roamed the property, acting as a watchdog.

Roberts's parents were considered eccentric by local residents. The couple had three children: David, Robert, and Linda. Robert would grow up to be a killer. Though the development of serial killers is imprecisely understood, there is usually a toxic combination of neglect and abuse in their backgrounds.

His mother, Louise "didn't pay attention to her teeth and eventually most of them rotted out. She lost most of her hair and covered the remaining wisps with a kerchief. Her chin sprouted so many hairs she developed a little goatee." Her husband, Leonard, was sixteen years older than Louise. He, like all the

---

[10] Thomas Ligotti. *My Work is Not Yet Done*. 65.

[11] Trevor Greene. *Bad Date. The Lost Girls of Vancouver's Low Track*. ECW Press, 2001. 142.

[12] Steve Cameron, "*On the Farm*," Vintage Canada 2011. 19.

Picktons, was remembered for his filthy appearance and an eye-watering stench of pig manure. The odor was "piercing and foul, clogging the back of your throat, and sticking like scum to your hair and skin." Neighbors claimed that as a child, "Willie used to crawl into the carcasses of gutted hogs to hide from people who were angry with him."[13]

As an adult, Robert helped run the family farm. In 1995 he and his brother Dave refurbished a corrugated metal shed "with enough tables and chairs to seat more than 150 people. They installed old beer signs, fluorescent light, a revolving disco ball and a sound system."[14] Their new business was christened the Piggy Palace Good Times Society. It became known for wild parties and raves that attracted up to 2,000 people.

These gatherings were a strange mixture of people ranging from Hells Angels members to local off-duty cops and city officials.[15] Sex workers from the DTES were brought to these parties. Many were never seen again. Pickton confessed to killing 49 of them. Talking with an undercover officer, he expressed regret at being caught before he could make his body count an even 50.

Bodies of the deceased were fed to the farm's hogs. It was also feared that Pickton had ground some of the victims up and mixed their flesh with pork products he sold to the public.

Despite the eventual capture of Pickton, women continue to disappear in the Downtown Eastside. Proof that predators are still operating in the area can be found in the newsletter for Vancouver sex workers called "Bad Date." This weekly flyer contains firsthand accounts, called in by sex workers, of ongoing violence and kidnapping attempts. Descriptions of perpetrators are given to warn women of possible attack. What is most disturbing is the sheer volume, week after week, of these violent encounters. Of course, kidnap attempts that

---

[13] Ibid. 8-9.

[14] Ibid. 133.

[15] Ibid. 136.

are successful go unreported and the actual number of women who go missing is unknown. One expects, at any moment, to come upon a sign reading: *MY WORK IS NOT YET DONE.*

If you spend any amount of time in the DTES and gain the confidence of its denizens, you will begin to hear stories. Whispered rumors, strange tidbits of gossip, unearthly hallucinations, and bizarre personal experiences will be related to you.

There is a widespread belief that the government is trying to kill the Downtown Eastside population by poisoning the drug supply. One man is sure there are invisible bats clinging to his body. There is talk of more missing women and sightings of old associates of Willy Pickton skulking about the neighborhood. Many believe Willy was a fall guy for other killers, who continue to prey on local sex workers. Others claim to have fought in underground clubs, where the wealthy pay to see men savage each other. Some say they have seen torture chambers and hidden places where strange idols are worshiped.[16]

Maybe these are simply the ramblings of drug addicts and madmen. Who are we to pass judgement? Can we, without undergoing years of psychic torment and drug induced delirium, determine what sort of reality these people perceive? In the words of Dr. Locrian: "What things had they seen… to give them such… wisdom?"

To release so many patients from the care of psychiatric hospitals and place them in the Downtown Eastside seems very much in keeping with the philosophy of Thomas Ligotti's fictional doctor. For Dr. Locrian's "ambition

---

[16] Shawn Phelps. Taken from the author's personal interviews while working as a psychiatric nurse in the Downtown Eastside.

led him not to relieve his patient's madness, but to exasperate it, — to let it breathe with a life of its own."[17] The filthy lanes and hotels of the Downtown Eastside seem to have been designed as the perfect laboratory where Ligotti's mad doctor could carry out his experiments.

Locrian's "proper treatment" for the mentally ill has been put into practice in the area. The daily scramble for survival in this atrocious neighborhood puts them through his prescribed "battery of hellish ordeals". Those who enter the area feel a sense of unease, of strangeness.

In *The Conspiracy Against the Human Race*, Thomas Ligotti captured the essence of what one experiences in the neighborhood: "there is a feeling of wrongness. A violation has transpired that alarms our internal authority regarding how something is supposed to happen or exist or behave." [18] It is a place where Mr. Ligotti's fictional worlds seem to have come to life.

---

[17] Thomas Ligotti, *Songs of a Dead Dreamer*, 195.

[18] Thomas Ligotti. *The Conspiracy Against the Human Race*. Penguin Books, 2018. 71-72.

BIBLIOGRAPHY

Cameron, Steve. *On the Farm*. Vintage Canada, 2011.

Cooper, David. *Practice in Mental Health-Substance Abuse*. Radcliffe Publishing Ltd, 2011.

Greene, Trevor. *Bad Date. The Lost Girls of Vancouver's Low Track*. ECW Press, 2001.

Little, Simon. "World's First Biometric Opioid Vending Machine." Global News, January 17, 2020.

Ligotti, Thomas. *The Conspiracy Against the Human Race*. Penguin Books, 2018.

—. *Songs of a Dead Dreamer and Grimscribe*. Penguin Classics, 2015.

—. *My Work Is Not Yet Done*. Virgin Books, 2009.

Mate, Gabor MD. *In the Land of the Hungry Ghosts. Close Encounters with Addiction*." Vintage Canada, 2012.

Rank, Otto. Quoted in *The Denial of Death*. Becker, Ernest." The Free Press, 2001.

Steffenhagen, Janet. "Our Four Blocks of Hell." *Vancouver Sun*, December 8, 2006.

A WILD GREEN TIDE IS SOON COMING — NOTES ON A PLANNED STORY

Jonathan Louis Duckworth

BECAUSE EVERY TROPE must be resisted, and because a triangle is a stronger shape than a star, there are only three, not five teenagers in the banana-yellow Jeep. First to be introduced is the unfortunately named Carlsbad—"Bad Carl" to his friends—whose appearance and ethnicity the writer leaves open, except that his hair grows as an unruly, dark crown. He chews on dip as the Jeep judders and bounces on the dirt road that split off from the highway that knits Calrose, Florida to the little gas-station-hamlet of Oliff Branch. Bad Carl hates dip, that much is clear from the face he makes if this is a movie, whereas if this is not a movie the prose relates in pithy strokes of narration the bitter, pungent expectations of North Florida country boys.

When the Jeep, artfully spattered with mud, pulls up, the driver is the first to get out and step into the shadow of the grim and gothic Bellamy House. We hate Big Al as soon as we meet him, with his half-unbuttoned Banana Republic shirt (the writer has channeled all his distaste for the Prepneck kids—Preppy Rednecks—he knew in high school into a homunculus of obnoxious traits and attitudes that wears the name Big Al), his wavy bleach-blond surfer hair, and his perpetual sunburn that will make him look 40 by the time he's 23. We hate him even more when he pours out the dregs of his bottle of Keystone Lite and then flings it at the house that looms ahead, the missile smashing through a dusty pane on the second floor.

Now the hypotenuse of the lust triangle climbs out of the Jeep, her pink, coltish legs a stark contrast to the earthy tones of the dirt road beneath her sandals. Zoey ties her frizzy red hair with a hairband and wears thick librarian glasses. She scolds Big Al for his senseless vandalism. Big Al hooks his arm around her waist and pulls her close to him to plant a sloppy kiss. In prose, Bad Carl watches the kiss and remembers when he and Zoey went to Dillon's Arcade for her ninth birthday party, and then thinks what a tragedy it is that someone as smart as her is letting her grades go to shit and wasting time with Big Al, forsaking nursing school for a future of stretch-marks and TV dinners and bags upon bags of crushed aluminum cans taken out to the curb every week. Meanwhile in a screen treatment, an extreme closeup on Bad Carl's eyes conveys his disgust and ambiguous jealousy.

Bad Carl tries one last time to talk Big Al out of the planned mischief. The usual reasons; cops, Judeo-Christian morality, respect for sufferers of suicidal depression like Mr. Bellamy. Big Al refutes and/or dismisses his concerns with practiced competence. The police don't ever come out here unless someone calls them, and anyway the land belongs to Big Al's dad—it'll be knocked down soon so he can build a new hunting lodge. What difference will a few more broken windows make?

Bad Carl attempts another tack—someone could get hurt.

What are you, a pussy?

Call me a pussy again, Alphonse.

Big Al's chapped lips are shaping the word when Zoey calls the boys' attention.

Out in the unruly woods, a whitetail buck is watching them from between two skinny slash pines. A beautiful eight-pointer, the kind of deer men parade from the beds of their trucks to show the world they get to decide when and how beautiful things depart.

A Wild Green Tide Is Soon Coming—Notes on a Planned Story

The deer shows no fear of the three teens, and stands stock still while watching them, an antlered harbinger to the terror that all such stories as this must deliver. Bad Carl thinks he sees a green glimmer in its eyes, while Big Al squints and pantomimes pointing a rifle at the animal.

The deer turns from them and calmly slinks back into the woods. The teens don't speak of it, or maybe they do, it depends on word economy up to this point (if a prose story) or various factors in a screen treatment.

Inside the house, fading afternoon light shunts in through cracks and holes, while cobwebs trace beautiful, elegiac veils around the chandelier light fixtures and the long-forgotten chairs of the parlor. In a film version, the camera pans past old, framed photos of the Bellamy family, some in black-and-white or sepia, including one of a bald man dressed in strange particolored robes. In prose, Bad Carl notices the photos but doesn't dwell on these pointillistic narrative particles. Speaking of the holes in the walls, Zoey asks aloud—and goes unanswered—if it's termites that create all the little puncture wounds peppering the walls.

We follow Bad Carl as he goes off on his own to explore the home. There is still plenty of light infiltrating the home, but he uses the flashlight on his phone and minds his steps as he ascends the creaking staircase. Maybe this is the time we learn more about Bad Carl's past and his character. Or maybe Bad Carl remains a cypher because the writer likes him that way. Maybe interiority and backstory are extraneous to the real meat and gristle of narrative, optional choices made *de rigueur* by decades of homogenized workshop instruction relying on canned aphorisms like "give every character one interesting, memorable physical trait." All of this is tentative, all of this is ephemeral, all of this may never get past the strobing black line at the top of the white word processor page.

Bad Carl follows a harsh glare into a room on the second floor, one cluttered with mirrors. Dusty and fogged and tarnished, but some still cast Bad Carl's face back at him, albeit altered in subtle or grotesque ways. Past the gauntlet of mirrors Bad Carl finds a bookcase stuffed with paperbacks with peeling spines, and next to that bookcase is a mechanical typewriter on a writing desk. A cobweb whorl surrounds it, as if some spider wove a ward around the machine. A single yellowed page sits atop the paper rest. Someone has typed a single line: A WILD GREEN TIDE IS SOON COMING.

A sound attracts his attention. Something taps the broken window, and a serpentine shadow slithers behind the illumed drapes. Bad Carl almost stumbles on a bottle—the bottle Big Al chucked—and when he looks up the shadow is gone.

Cut to another room if this is a visual form like film or a graphic novel, or possibly an RPG-maker indie horror game you can download for $2.99. If this remains prose fiction, Bad Carl overhears the other two and investigates the sounds they're making.

In this other room, what appears to be a trophy room—bursting with mounted sport fish, stuffed heads, and waterfowl hung from wires as if they're still flying—Big Al and Zoey are making out, Big Al with gusto, as if he's biting into a juicy nectarine, while Zoey is more tentative, her bespectacled eyes roving around and alighting on the sharp antlers and the glass eyes of the game animals, and the rusted, gossamer-wreathed barrels of shotguns and hunting rifles.

Big Al slides his hand up her stomach to lifts her cropped shirt, uncovering her bra and a mild red rash on the skin of her ribcage. Bad Carl walks in. Zoey's eyes meet his before Big Al notices him standing in the doorway.

Wordless tension, punctured by descriptions of Bad Carl's metabolic responses—something not too cliched hopefully, nothing about "boiling blood"—before Bad Carl turns around and walks away.

Carl, Zoey manages to say, but he's already gone.

Bad Carl returns to the mirrors. The sun has fallen beneath the pines, sky ruddy now, bloodshot and darkening to a bruise. In the rapidly darkening space Bad Carl finds Big Al's bottle and picks it up. He faces his nearest mirror-self, a dusty, warped semblance, and flings the bottle through it. Delicate mirror shatters against the sturdiness of mass-produced brown glass. In the immediate aftermath, something taps the window. Tap-tap-tap. Like a person's finger. But when Bad Carl investigates and peels aside the tattered drapes, there's nothing behind the window, only a lush air potato vine that's crawled up the house's face.

Bad Carl's own bewildered, frightened face stares back at him from a dozen tarnished silver puddles. Picking up the bottle again, Bad Carl smashes every surface where his face dares see him, and as he breaks mirror after mirror, he thinks back to childhood again, shared birthday parties with Zoey, bug hunts in the fields and pine woods outside the middle school, simpler days when they weren't expected to be anything but friends, when they both hated Big Al and his shithead land-developing, wetland-draining, pillar-of-the-community dad. This sudden flourish of interiority works in prose, while in a screen treatment the shots of mirrors splintering are interspersed with micro flashbacks of halcyon childhood times with Zoey before she took up with a boy who hates her only a little less than he hates himself.

In the last intact shard of a broken mirror, Bad Carl sees Big Al watching him from the doorway.

Blue balls work up a fury, don't they?

Fuck you.

Bet you'd like that.

Bad Carl balls up his fists, ready to speak the only language his family and community cared for him to learn fluently.

Big Al steps into the room, his muddy boots crunching over shards of glass. Bad Carl squares up, ready to drop his sunburnt ass.

From downstairs, Zoey calls up to the boys, Hey guys, something weird's going on here.

They don't answer or even acknowledge what she's said, like two opposed magnets on an inexorable course. The writer worries Zoey might be "flat," or "passive," or that she "lacks agency." Maybe she, like too many women or girls, is created only to be sacrificed—like the deer harbinger, only a token of terror. But then the writer remembers "agency" is a buzzword, a conversation filler in workshops that can't meet a story where it wants to be. What if she's here because it seemed as good or bad as any other choice? What if she couldn't imagine a life less empty than what her parents live, and her being here, forgotten by the men supposedly fighting over her, is just the inevitable result of that fatalism? Or maybe the writer gives himself too much credit.

Either way, back to the duel that isn't a duel, Bad Carl's all squared up for a fight, except Big Al doesn't want to fight.

She tell you it was my idea to invite you out here?

It's the only thing he could have said that Bad Carl isn't ready for. Just like he isn't ready when Big Al steps closer, his breath like the bottom of a beer bottle, his hair and skin redolent with styling mousse and sunscreen. Bad Carl's immobilized. He can't hear his own thoughts, let alone the slither of something serpentine crawling through the broken glass. He can't control the flow of his own blood, can't control the sudden burning heat in his ears or the tumescing cock in his jeans that even now his childhood nemesis's rough hand is digging under his belt for.

But then the scream. In prose, Bad Carl thinks of the time his uncle ran over a cat and it took ten minutes to die. In a graphic novel, the vowels—bold, embossed, red orange—splatter across the panels. In a film treatment, the actress who wears Zoey's skin dredges up every cubic inch of air in her lungs to let loose a queen of a scream.

The writer worries again about Zoey, not if she'll live (he knows better), but if there's enough of a character for anyone to care. He also worries, with Aristotle breathing over his shoulder, if the story lacks a sufficient anagnorisis, and if this lack is why he hasn't finished it. Is there no wheel or reversal, no sparkling recognition to exert its fascination on the audience? Unless the anagnorisis already came, before the "monster" even showed up, or unless the recognition comes not between two characters but between the characters and the setting (realizing this world doesn't want them) or between the characters

A Wild Green Tide Is Soon Coming—Notes on a Planned Story

and the narrative itself, when they realize what genre this is too late to save their friend.

The boys scramble down the stairs, enmity and eros dissolved, but in the rapidly occluding parlor their phone flashlights find no sign of Zoey, only eight long, jagged crimson streaks, the grooves her fingers carved into the floorboards as they were ground to pulp by an irresistible force. The front door hangs ajar, rattling on its rusted hinges while the dark jaws of the universe lurk beyond its frame.

Bad Carl is the first to rush out and shout Zoey's name, and in answer Zoey screams again, somewhere out there, somewhere in the trees. Bad Carl and Big Al call again, but they've heard the last of Zoey. The only reply is the rustle and squirm of something among the trees, a leafy susurrus most of the way to being laughter.

Only now do the two young men—little boys lost—notice how the vines swathed over the Bellamy house are moving, tendrils snaking in every direction.

They argue, both conscious of the menace all around them, but at cross-purposes on what to do. Big Al wants to get the hell out of here and drive back to Calrose where things make sense (the *Ordinary World*, if we're riding with Campbell and all his confirmation bias, and we'd prefer not to). But Bad Carl thinks they should search for Zoey, hoping against hope there's still something left of her to find and save. He has passion, courage, and morals on his side. But Big Al has the keys, and more importantly, Big Al isn't afraid to save his own sunburnt ass whatever it takes. He shoves Bad Carl and makes a dash for his Jeep. Bad Carl catches him by his ankle and Big Al falls.

A melee ensues, a grapple for the keys. Knees, elbows, teeth, blows below the belt, all on offer here, while all around them the kudzu (three-pronged, voracious), muscadine (spade-shaped, cunning), and air potato vines (round, sturdy) slither from their dark marches beneath the slash pines.

Big Al comes out the victor. Two things can happen depending on which the writer finds more convincing when he actually sits down to write this in-scene. Either Big Al escapes from the scrum, or he really starts giving it to Bad Carl, hammering him with blows or choking him. Either way, the vines intercede. In scenario one they snag Big Al's ankle just as he's almost to the Jeep, while in scenario two they wrap around his waist and lift him. In both cases, vines enter through the mouth and nostrils, through new orifices they create in his ribs and back. They wriggle through every soft passage and branch their tendrils in search of something new and interesting. A medically fascinating vivisection from the vines' perspective, but from Bad Carl's view on the ground it's like watching high tension steel cables shred through a blood bag.

Anointed with his nemesis/would-be paramour's blood, Bad Carl is lucky that the keys fall into his hand. He runs for the Jeep while the vines are still sorting through Big Al's parts as a watchmaker puzzles over a clock's complications. The Jeep roars, and the radio that had been playing Pantera when the teens arrived now blares static. In his panic, Bad Carl doesn't pay any attention to this little detail.

Even as Bad Carl turns the Jeep around and angles it toward the dirt road—that humble, ruddy viaduct to civilization—the vines swarm over the Bellamy house and over the lawn. Under their mass the old house groans, shudders, collapses, decades of lost memories and old secrets imploded in an instant, its serried phantoms made homeless, condemned to wander the unpeopled wilderness.

The vines make a go at the Jeep, and an enterprising shock of muscadine wraps around its bumper but only manages to tear off a plank of chrome as the vehicle charges toward freedom.

In prose, Bad Carl's lack of interiority is the writer's boon now—terror is the hardest emotion to convey, except by direct action, and here Bad Carl's mind-numbing fear manifests in him nearly driving Big Al's Jeep into a ditch while he stares uncomprehending at his phone, trying to remember his own passcode before he realizes he doesn't need the code to call 911.

Call the cops and tell them what? He doesn't know, and it's just as well because he doesn't have service anyway. In the filmed version, a high-altitude tracking shot follows the Jeep, a garish yellow beacon blazing through the benighted arteries of the vast North Florida pine flatwoods, while in prose Bad Carl observes the silhouettes of trees shuddering as he bullets past them, off the dirt path and onto the paved state road.

Bad Carl drives without a destination in mind. Anywhere but where he's coming from. Eventually a gas station appears from the nightscape, brightly lit, a bastion of commerce and civilization out in the suddenly hostile wild.

There are no other cars in sight, something he barely notices as he pulls up, just as he hasn't really noticed that the radio is still shedding a froth of static even though he's closer to Calrose now, almost on its outskirts.

Bad Carl leaves the engine on and rushes for the door. Of course we know how this ends—civilization's glow never chases the monster away: at best the light of a watchman's lantern or the cone of a streetlight buys the hero some time. At worst, the light is like the phosphorescent lure of an angler fish.

The door doesn't open, and Bad Carl jostles the handle and pounds the glass barrier before he notices the button to the side of the door labeled *Please Ring for Entry After Dark*. He rings the bell, once, twice, thrice, but nothing happens.

Inside the gas station hot dogs turn on a cooker, the slushy mixers churn, one-gallon cans of "authentic, local" boiled peanuts gather dust. But no one's inside to let him in.

Bad Carl wonders what that means, wonders why he still has no service, and as he's trying and failing to process his predicament, the gas station's lights flicker and then fail. Bad Carl runs to the Jeep while vines reach out from the forest. He shifts into drive as muscadines twine around the concrete pillars that support the station's canopy, and a kudzu strand tears off the driver side mirror.

Bad Carl drives, toward nothing, toward a town that may not exist anymore. Drives because there's nothing else he can do, no one he can go back to save, no one he can call for help.

The way ahead, the Jeep's high beams shine off the dewy edges of lush leaves, while in the rearview mirror twin onslaughts of vines swallow the road, erasing the black scar humans burned through nature.

Up ahead same as behind. The vines close in, spill out from the woods that hem either side of the road. Bad Carl can do nothing but scream, an angry, defiant roar that cracks and stumbles into something small, something plaintive. Why me, the scream asks, why any of us? As far as the writer is concerned, every revenge story centers on a consequentialist moral argument, but this argument can assume two divergent forms. The first: *X Did Y, So Must Suffer Z*. The second: *I Don't Care If X Did Y Or Not, I'll Exact My Z On Them*. This is the second kind of revenge story, where the X is the world's ghost/nature's hauntology/anima mundi in the form of animate vines, Y is the three teens selected as representatives of the human race, and Z is a balancing of the scales, a hard reset to default settings. Heavy-handed? Oh yes.

A wild green tide washes over the Jeep and Bad Carl within it.

Cut to black. Epilogue time. Bright light of morning glistens off dew rolling down the curve of a vine's leaf. Pan down to a verdant forest floor, a crisscross lattice of various vines protecting the callow saplings of a new global carbon sink. Pan up. Three pairs of dirty human feet tread softly over the tender vines. A sun rises, and three young naked people, two boys and one girl, glimpsed only from behind, explore an Edenic paradise of majestic greenery, where vines of impossible dimensions branch into explosions of voluptuous flowers and succulent fruit of every color.

Above, a black monolith strobes in a tract of white.

Learning Process

Andrew Wilbur

Recently I've been learning from my dreams. They're helping me – teaching me - to confront the fact that I'm controlling and possessive. Really, it's just one dream, elongated with each repetition. I've learned its lesson, so I think I've now reached the final scene.

It begins with you waking up, angry at me. We're in a cabin or a lodge, in quiet isolation on the most beautiful island on Earth. That's not just my opinion - the island is famous for its topographical anomalies and remarkable wildlife and is justifiably swarming with tourists. We see them when we leave our secluded lodge, faceless little ants that crowd our views of the sea and mountains. But there are so many hidden areas of the island that the tourists don't know about, and this is where you and I spend our days, your anger gradually lifting as I guide you through pockets of singular beauty. I know the situation is precarious. I could easily lose your trust by saying the wrong thing. I want to ask you the Big Question, but I'm patient.

Impulsiveness is one of my faults, so I work hard to hold everything steady, careful to compromise when necessary, making sure you can take the lead now and again, and suppressing an urge to disagree even when I know

I'm right. It's working. By afternoon you're smiling. We walk together, alone, through a narrow gorge whose walls are slanted at impossible angles, causing strange reverberations when we speak. We visit the "animated beach," where thousands of black crabs scurry around identically colored chunks of petrified lava, producing an illusion of vibrating, shapeshifting rock. We marvel at the thick, blue, iridescent worms that cling to trees in the remote forest near our lodge. You love nature, intellectually and spiritually. You can explain the science of everything that we witness in a way that doesn't detract from its mystique. To my surprise, you even show some interest in visiting The Tower when I suggest a trip there.

I haven't given you any details about what's inside. Intuitively you seem to understand that clambering around an old factory is dangerous, but your curiosity is insatiable. The problem is, I don't like to think about The Tower in my dreams. When a dream about you starts tilting toward The Tower, there's a real risk of it becoming another kind of dream, one where I move into an empty warehouse or a deserted hotel. In these dreams I'm comfortable at first, grateful for the space and solitude that these places offer. I find an old blanket, maybe even a bed, and use a little dark corner as a base for my wanderings. Inevitably, though, I realize that I'm not alone. And the dreams turn very bad when I discover who else is in the building with me. But the worst part always comes later. It happens when I realize that I'm not simply a visitor or an explorer, that *this is where I live*, and I'm never going to leave.

In time I've worked up the courage to ask the Big Question. I know there's a chance that you'll react badly to it, and I'm also nervous about how I might react to your answer. It's getting close to sunset, and we emerge from one of the underground tunnels where luminescent insects flicker and flash, lighting the way for us. You run to the top of a steep hill, laughing as I try and fail to catch up. As we reach the summit, the sound of a Christmas choir rises to meet us.

The choir is for tourists, you tell me. Indeed, down below we can see a huge agglomeration of bodies stretching from the base of the hill toward the seafront where the choir sings. You smile: I still kind of like it, though. Did you remember that it's Christmas? I smile back, a confession that the moment, however schmaltzy, hasn't left me unmoved.

Far past the mass of tourists, behind another set of hills that frame a distant curve of the shoreline, I spot little rosy lights flashing on The Tower. The sun hasn't set, but it seems as if that part of the island is already dark. I figure that you could see it if you tried, but I don't want your attention there.

The signals from The Tower seem like an invitation, or at least a confirmation that this is the right moment. Sit down, I say. We lower ourselves, as if settling in for a picnic. Your face is covered in shadow now, and I've never been more possessed by it. I don't hesitate: Why did you go, and where have you been all this time?

You look away, then stand up and turn your back to me. I follow but say nothing, just watch you stare into a perfect sphere of flaming red sun. I remember how you once explained the astronomical mechanics that allowed people to look directly at the sun at certain times of the day, but only from specific elevations on the island. I watch you with all the intensity that you fix on the sun, but soon you're gone.

It's dark now, and I'm jogging down the hill, toward the seafront, pushing past tourists who've lost all individual distinction and are literally faceless, just blank surfaces like the blackest obsidian, balanced on identical stick-bodies. I walk and walk, following the summons of The Tower. I haven't found you by the time I notice that I'm back in the city, a place as fetid and corrupt as you are pure. The realization is devastating. I long to be back in the forests and gorges, carefully calculating a rejoinder to one of your effortless jokes. But I'm standing in the midst of the city at the entrance of a decrepit former factory with an enormous smokestack, the place that I call The Tower, and it's cold here.

Its flashing red lights suffuse the whole scene, alternating with swirls of blue. The effect is disorienting until other objects come into focus and I see that I'm surrounded by police cars and ambulances. A cordon has been formed around the building with yellow police tape. Across from me, two paramedics load a police officer into the back of an ambulance. He lies unconscious on a stretcher, breathing through an oxygen mask, blood soaking the sheet that covers his torso. As I approach the cordon an officer lifts up the tape and motions for me to duck under. My foot knocks the head of a different body, immobile and unresponsive, covered completely by a white sheet, waiting to be hauled away. This earns a scowl from the cop, who gestures to the entrance of The Tower, where another officer waits, glaring at me. I try to appear helpful, striding confidently to the man who appears to be in charge of this whole operation.

I cast a final look back toward the other side of the cordon, away from the factory. I'm searching for you, of course, but I know you're gone. Next to the body that I accidentally kicked, another one lies on a stretcher. Several cops have gathered around the ambulance, some taking long looks in my direction. I feel a sharp grip on my arm.

You come here, says the chief officer. We're standing directly in front of the factory's large metal door, the one with the broken locks that enabled my first entry to this place. Bruises linger on my bicep when he finally lets go. You know why you're here? he asks. I'm learning now, I say. These dreams have been helping me. I can be very needy and possessive. Controlling! And impulsive – a bad combination.

He's been holding something in his other hand, which he now reveals: a police badge, smeared with blood. He points to one of the body bags. You know who that is?

My dreams have been helping me, I repeat. I don't need this. I understand everything.

Let me tell you his name. He had a family. And on Christmas, you piece of shit...

The cop's breath smells of cold water and pumps out of him in little clouds, like human chimney. He leans in close to my ear but says nothing. Instead he kisses me softly on the cheek. His whiskers scratch my skin, and his breath leaves a little patch of heat, as if I've rubbed my face against an itchy woolen blanket.

Now I'm indoors and it's become one of the other dreams. One of the ones with lots of dark, empty rooms in a forgotten structure that feels, at first, as if it belongs only to me. And I'll spend a long time feeling that way. But eventually others will arrive and the situation will turn very dire. That's when I'll want to leave. But when I can't do that I'll need to confront another uncomfortable fact: *I live here now.*

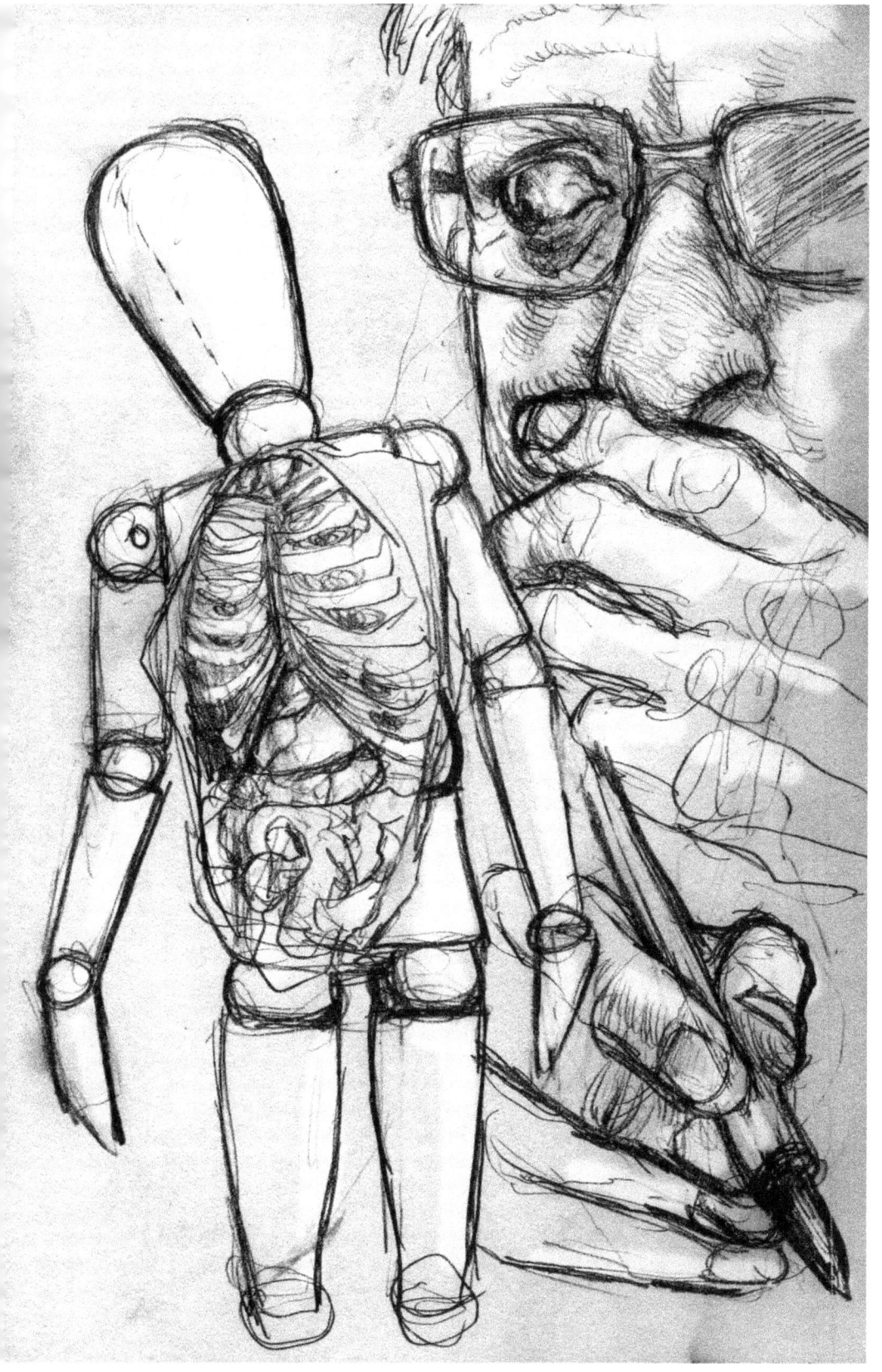

CONTRIBUTORS

Rebecca Allred is the author of numerous stories, including: "When Dark-Eyed Ophelia Sings" (Nightscript III); "Lambda 580" (*A Walk on the Weird Side*); "The Last Plague Doctor" (Borderlands 6); and the novella *And In Her Smile, The World* (with Gordon B. White). In addition to writing, she enjoys collecting books, spending sunny mornings in her backyard, and painting. Rebecca lives in Central Oregon with her spouse, four cats, and a one giant dog.

César Dávila Andrade (Cuenca, 1918—Caracas, 1967) was an Ecuadorian poet, short fiction writer, and essayist. He was known as El Fakir for both his physical appearance and the mystical and esoteric concerns of his work. His chronicle of atrocities and forced labor under Spanish rule, "Bulletin and Elegy of the Mitas," is widely acclaimed, both critically and popularly, as a key text of 20th century Ecuadorian poetry.

Michael Bailey is a recipient of the Bram Stoker Award (and nine-time nominee), Benjamin Franklin Award, and a five-time Shirley Jackson Award nominee. He has authored numerous novels, novellas, novelettes, and fiction & poetry collections. Recent work includes *Agatha's Barn*, a tie-in novella to Josh Malerman's *Carpenter's Farm*, a collaborative novella with Erinn L. Kemper called *The Call of the Void*, and *Sifting the Ashes*, a collaborative and lengthy poetry collection with Marge Simon. He runs the small press Written Backwards and has edited and published numerous anthologies, such as *The Library of the Dead, the Chiral Mad* series, and *Miscreations: Gods, Monstrosities & Other Horrors*. He lives in Costa Rica where he is rebuilding his life after surviving one of the most catastrophic wildfires in California history.

Paul L. Bates began writing in earnest over sixty years ago. He is especially proud of his publication credits in *Vastarien, A Literary Journal*, and wishes to thank Jon Padgett once again for inviting him along for the ride, and Thomas Ligotti for his inestimable source of inspiration. Fantasy or reality, he hopes the journey will eventually continue...

M.E. Bronstein is an academic who likes to explore (and/or muddle) intersections between scholarship and fiction. She studies medieval translations of Ovid and writes various kinds of horror and dark fantasy. Her short fiction has appeared in *Beneath Ceaseless Skies*, *PodCastle*, *khōréō magazine*, and elsewhere.

Laura Cranehill is a writer based in Portland Oregon, where she lives with her partner and three sons. Her work has been published in *Abyss & Apex*, *Strange Horizons*, and *The Future Fire*.

Jonathan Louis Duckworth is a completely normal, entirely human person with the right number of heads and everything. He received his MFA from Florida International University and his PhD from University of North Texas. He is the author of *Have You Seen the Moon Tonight? & Other Rumors* (JournalStone Publishing) and his speculative fiction work appears in

Pseudopod, Fantasy & Science Fiction, Beneath Ceaseless Skies, Southwest Review, and elsewhere. He is an active HWA member.

Dave Felton's scratchboard illustrations have appeared in books published by Chiroptera Press, Broken Eye Books, Dim Shores, Dunhams Manor Press, *Vastarien*, and *The Lovecraft eZine*.

Richard Gavin's writing explores the nexus of dread and the numinous. His horror fiction has been collected in six volumes, including *grotesquerie* (Undertow Publications, 2020). He has also authored works of esotericism for distinguished venues such as Theion Publishing and Three Hands Press. Richard resides in Ontario, Canada.

Chris Kuriata lives in and often writes about the Niagara Region. His short fiction has appeared in magazines in Canada, the US, the UK, Ireland, Australia, New Zealand, South Africa, and Japan. His novel *Sacrifice of the Sisters Lot* was published by Palimpsest Press in October 2023.

Ben Larned (he/they) is a queer horror writer, filmmaker and educator. His work is featured in *Vastarien*, Creepy Podcast, *Dose of Dread* and *Seize the Press*, among others. "What Scares a Ghost?", his story in Coffin Bell, was nominated for the Best Small Fictions 2023. His short film "Payment" is streaming on ALTER. He holds an MFA from The New School.

Carl Lavoie likes marginalia, the emblems of Alciato, faces in wainscoting, and not being sure whether something happens to his waking or dreaming self. He lives in Southwestern Ontario.

Adam Lawrence's poetry has recently appeared in *Misfitmagazine, SurVision Magazine,* and *Carousel Magazine.* Lawrence works as a freelance copyeditor and writer in Florenceville-Bristol, NB, the French Fry Capital of the World.

Romana Lockwood is a lady, and ladies do not reveal their age. Her many incarnations have included nurse in a devastating war, typist, war correspondent, television news anchor, housewife, waitress, and columnist. Her column "In My Eyes," which ran from 19_ to 20_ was, in the eyes of many, a serious contender for the Pulitzer Prize, or at the very least the Horace Greeley or the Breindel awards. Her first marriage was to Ernest James Hayden, a shoe salesman, who passed in 19_ from a failure of the heart, the variety that physicians refer to as "massive." Of her second marriage she does not speak. She rejects in toto the Abrahamic religions. She takes daily walks, her coffee black, her cats calico, and her tea sweet.

Emma E. Murray's stories have appeared in anthologies like *What One Wouldn't Do, Obsolescence,* and *Ooze: Little Bursts of Body Horror* as well as magazines such as *CHM, Pyre,* and *If There's Anyone Left.* Her debut chapbook *Exquisite Hunger* is available from Medusa Haus.

Shawn Phelps studied Anthropology at the University of Chicago. After leading a series of expeditions in the Amazon, he was elected to The Explorer's Club. His work has been published in *Chthonic Matter, Penumbra, The Watsonian, Halloweenthology, Monster Fight at OK Corral, Vastarien, It's All in My Mind,* and *The Book of Monster Stories.* He works as an RN in a psychiatric intensive care unit at the Center for Addictions and Mental Health in Toronto.

Marisca Pichette is a queer author based in Massachusetts, on Pocumtuck and Abenaki land. Her work has appeared in *Strange Horizons, Clarkesworld, The Magazine of Fantasy & Science Fiction, Fantasy Magazine, Flash Fiction Online, PseudoPod, PodCastle*, and others. She is the winner of the 2022 *F(r)iction* Spring Literary Contest and has been nominated for the Best of the Net, Pushcart, Utopia, and Dwarf Stars awards. Her speculative poetry collection, *Rivers in Your Skin, Sirens in Your Hair*, is out now from Android Press.

Perry Ruhland is a writer based in Chicago. His writing has previously been published in *Baffling Magazine, The Cafe Irreal, Vastarien Magazine, Chthonic Matter Quarterly*, and ergot.press.

Dyani Sabin is a queer, Jewish author of speculative fiction, poetry, and science journalism. Her work has been published in *Strange Horizons, Enchanted Conversations, Vastarien*, and *Reckoning* as well as *Popular Science,* among others. She is the co-editor of *Music Information Literacy: Inclusion and Advocacy,* forthcoming from Library Juice Press in 2024. You can find her haunting a cornfield or chasing ghosts on the endangered species list.

Jonathan Simkins is the translator of *El Creacionismo* by Vicente Huidobro (The Lune). His translations of César Dávila Andrade have appeared in *Bennington Review*, *Chicago Review*, *Modern Poetry in Translation*, *Notre Dame Review*, *Tampa Review*, *The Journal*, and *Tinderbox Poetry Journal*.

Alyza Taguilaso is a resident doctor training in General Surgery in the Philippines. Her work has been shortlisted for a Rhysling Award and contests like the Manchester and Bridport Poetry prizes. Her poems have been published in several publications, including *Electric Literature, Crazy Horse, The Deadlands, Canthius, Fantasy Magazine, Strange Horizons, Orbis Journal, Voice and Verse,* and *Luna Journal PH*.

SJ Townend is an author of horror, sci-fi, speculative, and dark fiction. She's currently compiling her first collection of horror stories, *Sick Girl Screams,* which is to be published by Brigids Gate Press early 2024. SJ also has a contemporary romance, *Pick-Up Lines*, coming out with Champagne Book Group later this year. In her spare time, she helps run Bag of Bones Press.

Andrew Wilbur is an Associate Teaching Professor at Seoul National University in South Korea, where he helps to run the Extra Noir music label and organize experimental live music events. He has written two (unproduced) feature-length adaptations of Thomas Ligotti stories and plans to continue writing weird-fiction adaptations and original screenplays.

Carson Winter is an award-winning author, punker, and raw nerve. His fiction has been featured in *Apex, Vastarien,* and *Tales to Terrify.* "The Guts of

Myth" was published in volume one of Dread Stone Press' *Split Scream* series. His novella, *Soft Targets,* is out now from Tenebrous Press. He lives in the Pacific Northwest.